Mastering Data Science and Analytics

The Power of Data: From Analysis to Action in the Modern World

Finnley Harper

© Copyright 2024 - All rights reserved.

The content contained within this book may not be reproduced, duplicated or transmitted without direct written permission from the author or the publisher.

Under no circumstances will any blame or legal responsibility be held against the publisher, or author, for any damages, reparation, or monetary loss due to the information contained within this book, either directly or indirectly.

Legal Notice:

This book is copyright protected. It is only for personal use. You cannot amend, distribute, sell, use, quote or paraphrase any part, or the content within this book, without the consent of the author or publisher.

Disclaimer Notice:

Please note the information contained within this document is for educational and entertainment purposes only. All effort has been executed to present accurate, up to date, reliable, complete information. No warranties of any kind are declared or implied. Readers acknowledge that the author is not engaging in the rendering of legal, financial, medical or professional advice. The content within this book has been derived from various sources. Please consult a licensed professional before attempting any techniques outlined in this book.

By reading this document, the reader agrees that under no circumstances is the author responsible for any losses, direct or indirect, that are incurred as a result of the use of information contained within this document, including, but not limited to, errors, omissions, or inaccuracies.

Table of Contents

INTRODUCTION

Developing an awareness of data science and analytics is now crucial for businesses and individuals looking to stay creative and competitive in an era where data is growing exponentially. Your thorough guide to negotiating the complicated and ever-changing world of data is " Mastering Data Science and Analytics: The Power of Data: From Analysis to Action in the Modern World." Suppose you're a practiced professional seeking to expand your expertise or a novice keen to dive into this fascinating sector. In that case, this book offers the perspectives, resources, and practical applications you need to leverage the power of data properly.

Data science is gaining valuable insights from data to support strategic planning and well-informed decision-making. It goes beyond simple figure crunching. This book explores the fundamental ideas, sophisticated methods, and practical applications of data science and analytics. Each chapter will provide the tools you need to succeed, from comprehending data kinds and statistical principles to investigating machine learning methods and creating a data-driven culture.

As you go on this adventure, you'll learn how data science affects daily lives, changes industries, and determines business tactics. You'll learn how to transform unstructured data into actionable insights through real-world scenarios, case studies, and interactive projects. Greetings from a world where data is your most precious resource and can drive success and innovation.

CHAPTER I

Welcome to the Data Revolution

Importance of Data in the Modern World

Data has become an indispensable resource in today's world, transforming several industries and radically changing how we see and engage with the world. This shift, frequently called the "Data Revolution," is brought about by the previously unheard-of volume, speed, and diversity of data collected. It is impossible to overestimate the significance of data in the current world since it propels innovation, supports decision-making, and helps us comprehend complicated systems on a deeper level. The pervasiveness of data is profoundly and multidimensionally changing our lives, from augmenting public services to strengthening commercial tactics.

The Data Revolution is all about making informed decisions. Data analytics empowers businesses with crucial insights into consumer behavior, industry trends, and operational efficiency. By leveraging big data, businesses can gain a merciless edge by tailoring their legacy and resources to converge the unique needs of their customers. For instance, e-commerce behemoths like Amazon and Alibaba analyze enormous volumes of client data using sophisticated algorithms to provide tailored recommendations and improve inventory management. This data-driven strategy improves customer happiness and increases revenue growth and operational efficiency.

Data is essential to governance, public services, and the corporate world. Public institutions and governments use data to create policies, distribute funds, and assess the success of various initiatives. Data analytics, for instance, was crucial in tracking the COVID-19 pandemic's virus spread, locating hotspots, and developing focused interventions. Health authorities use data to control healthcare resources, forecast outbreaks, and notify the public about preventative actions. Data-driven insights are helpful in education for understanding student performance, identifying gaps in knowledge, and customizing curricula to enhance results. As a result, data is essential for advancing society and improving public welfare.

The Data Revolution greatly benefits the scientific community. By analyzing extensive databases, researchers can find patterns and make previously unthinkable discoveries in domains like astrophysics, climate science, and genomes. For example, the rapid development of personalized medicine and the finding of disease-causing genes in genomics have been facilitated by the availability of large amounts of genetic data. Climate scientists employ many data sources such as satellites, sensors, and simulations to gain insights into climate change, forecast extreme weather occurrences, and create mitigation and adaptation plans. Thus, scientific progress and our understanding of nature are fueled by the capacity to analyze and interpret large, complicated datasets.

Moreover, expert systems and artificial intelligence (AI) are two more fields in which data is crucial. For learning and prediction, these systems rely on large datasets. Intelligent retrieval (AI) systems, such as virtual assistants and self-driving cars, are fueled by data, which allows them to perform better over time. Algorithms for machine learning examine past data to find trends and make judgments with little assistance from humans. A few industries that stand to profit immensely from this potential are manufacturing, banking, and healthcare, as AI-driven insights boost accuracy, innovation, and productivity.

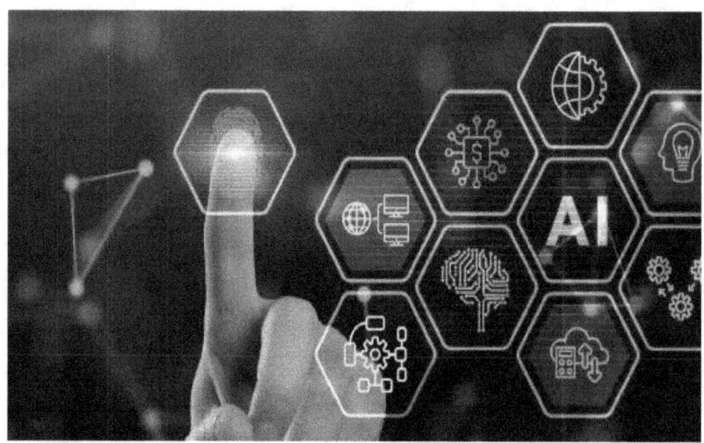

But the abundance of data also brings with it difficulties, especially when it comes to security and privacy. Data breaches and misuse are becoming more likely as data becomes increasingly essential to our daily lives. Preserving public confidence and guaranteeing the security of personal information is critical. Directives like the European Union have established data management and privacy protection guidelines, particularly the General Data Protection Regulation (GDPR). Conglomerates are required to implement robust security measures, comply with these laws regarding sensitive data, and minimize risks.

In conclusion, the modern world is being transformed by the Data Revolution. Data is essential because it may stimulate innovation, improve decision-making, and deepen our understanding of intricate systems. Data is a vital resource that drives advancement and development, from businesses and public services to scientific research and artificial intelligence (AI). We must address the issues raised by the growing generation and usage of data and ensure it is utilized sensibly and ethically. We may open up new possibilities and build a more knowledgeable, effective, and fair future by embracing the power of data.

Objectives of the Book

"Mastering Data Science and Analytics: The Power of Data: From Analysis to Action in the Modern World" is not just a book, it's a tool for empowerment. It seeks to give readers a thorough understanding of data science and its practical applications. In an era where data is the new oil, learning data science tools and methodologies is not just beneficial, it's essential for anybody trying to prosper in today's world. This book aims to bridge the gap between theoretical knowledge and real-world application by equipping readers with the skills and insights required to transform raw data into meaningful action, empowering them to navigate the data-driven world with confidence.

One of the book's primary goals is to explain the complexity of data science to a large audience. Whether you are an experienced expert looking to expand your knowledge or a newcomer to the industry, this book provides clear, concise explanations of fundamental concepts and approaches. By degrading complex ideas into digestible chunks, the book assures that readers can follow along and understand the material regardless of past knowledge. This approach is critical to making data science more accessible and encouraging more individuals to participate in this fast-developing field.

Another important goal of the book is to highlight the actual applications of data science in many industries. By maneuvering real-world examples and case studies, the book shows how data science can solve complicated challenges and create innovation. Readers will learn how several industries, including healthcare, finance, marketing, and logistics, use data science to optimize operations and achieve strategic goals. This not only demonstrates the versatility of data science, but it also inspires readers by showing them the potential impact of their work in their own professional settings.

The book also strives to promote a thorough awareness of the ethical issues and concerns linked with data science. As data becomes more integrated into our daily lives, concerns about privacy, security, and bias grow more pressing than ever. This book addresses these concerns by emphasizing the significance of ethical data practices and offering recommendations for responsible data management. By focusing on the ethical aspects of data science, the book reassures readers that they can take a principled approach to their work, ensuring that the benefits of data-driven decision-making are fulfilled without jeopardizing individual rights or social values.

Furthermore, the book aims to provide readers with hands-on experience via practical projects and activities. Theory is vital, but the genuine value of data science is found in its implementation. Each chapter offers practical examples and exercises to help readers apply what they've learned and improve their skills. By completing these tasks, readers can acquire confidence in their talents and create a work portfolio showcasing their data science expertise. This practical focus guarantees that even more readers seize the concepts but may also devote them to the real world. Settings.

The book's primary goal is to lay a solid foundation in data science's fundamental principles and methodologies. Topics covered include data collection, cleaning, and preprocessing; exploratory data analysis; statistical approaches; machine learning; and data visualization. By addressing these critical areas, the book provides a firm foundation for readers to build as they delve further into specific themes or pursue advanced studies. The detailed covering of core issues guarantees readers grasp the entire data science pipeline, from raw data to actionable insights.

Finally, the book seeks to instill a data-driven perspective in its readers. In today's data-driven society, the capacity to think critically about data and use it to make decisions is an important skill. This book urges readers to take a data-driven approach to their personal and professional lives, cultivating a culture of curiosity, analytical thinking, and ongoing learning. The book promotes a data-driven approach, which helps readers grasp the revolutionary potential of data science and pushes them to stay current on the latest advances.

Finally, "Mastering Data Science and Analytics: The Power of Data: From Analysis to Action in the Modern World" seeks to provide a complete, accessible, and practical introduction to data science. By demystifying complex concepts, emphasizing real-world applications, addressing ethical concerns, providing hands-on experience, laying a solid foundation, and inspiring a data-driven mindset, the book anticipates readers with the knowledge and skills they need to harness the power of data and make informed decisions in the modern world.

CHAPTER II

What is Data Science and Analytics?

Definitions and Key Concepts

In the realm of data science and analytics, understanding key definitions and concepts is essential for building a solid foundation of knowledge. Data science, often described as the intersection of statistics, computer science, and domain expertise, encompasses a wide range of techniques and methodologies for extracting insights from data. At its core, data science is about using data to answer questions, solve problems, and drive decision-making processes. Analytics, on the other hand, refers to the systematic exploration of data using statistical and computational techniques to uncover patterns, trends, and relationships. Together, data science and analytics form the backbone of modern-day decision-making, enabling organizations to derive actionable insights from vast amounts of data.

Central to the field of data science are the concepts of data types and data sources. Data can be categorized into two main types: structured and unstructured. Structured data is organized in a predefined format, such as tables in a relational database, making it easy to analyze and manipulate. Unstructured data, on the other hand, lacks a predefined structure and includes text, images, videos, and social media posts. Understanding the characteristics of different data types is crucial for determining the appropriate tools and techniques for analysis. Data can also be sourced from various internal and external sources, including databases, sensors, social media platforms, and web scraping. The availability of diverse data sources presents both opportunities and challenges for data scientists, who must navigate the complexities of data integration and data quality to ensure the reliability and validity of their analyses.

Another key concept in data science is the data lifecycle, which encompasses the processes of data collection, storage, processing, analysis, and interpretation. Each stage of the data lifecycle presents unique challenges and considerations that must be addressed to ensure the integrity and usefulness of the data. Data collection involves gathering data from various sources and formats, while data storage requires selecting appropriate databases or data warehouses to store the data securely. Data processing involves cleaning and preprocessing the data to remove errors and inconsistencies, while data analysis entails applying statistical and machine learning techniques to extract insights from the data. Finally, data interpretation involves translating the findings of the analysis into actionable recommendations or decisions. By understanding the data lifecycle, data scientists can effectively manage and leverage data throughout its lifecycle to derive meaningful insights.

One of the fundamental concepts in data science is exploratory data analysis (EDA), which involves visually exploring and summarizing data to uncover patterns, trends, and relationships. EDA techniques include descriptive statistics, data visualization, and dimensionality reduction, which enable data scientists to gain insights into the underlying structure of the data. Descriptive statistics, such as mean, median, and standard deviation, provide summary measures of central tendency and variability, while data visualization techniques, such as histograms, scatter plots, and heatmaps, offer intuitive ways to visualize and interpret complex datasets. Dimensionality reduction techniques, such as principal component analysis (PCA) and t-distributed stochastic neighbor embedding (t-SNE), help reduce the dimensionality of high-dimensional datasets while preserving their essential characteristics. By performing EDA, data scientists can identify outliers, detect patterns, and generate hypotheses for further analysis.

Machine learning is another key concept in data science, which involves the development of algorithms that can learn from data and make predictions or decisions without being explicitly programmed. Machine learning algorithms can be broadly categorized into supervised, unsupervised, and reinforcement learning, each with its unique characteristics and applications. Supervised learning involves training a model on labeled data to make predictions or classify new data points, while unsupervised learning involves clustering or dimensionality reduction to discover hidden patterns or structures in unlabeled data. Reinforcement learning, on the other hand, involves training an agent to interact with an environment and learn optimal decision-making strategies through trial and error. Machine learning algorithms have wide-ranging applications in fields such as healthcare, finance, marketing, and robotics, where they are used to automate tasks, make predictions, and optimize decision-making processes.

In conclusion, definitions and key concepts form the building blocks of data science and analytics, providing the necessary framework for understanding and analyzing data. By familiarizing themselves with concepts such as data types, data sources, the data lifecycle, exploratory data analysis, and machine learning, data scientists can effectively leverage data to derive insights and drive decision-making processes. As data continues to grow in volume and complexity, a solid understanding of key concepts is essential for navigating the challenges and opportunities of the data-driven world.

The Data Science Process

The data science process is a systematic approach to extracting insights and knowledge from data, encompassing a series of steps that guide the analysis and interpretation of data. At its core, the data science process is iterative and flexible, allowing data scientists to adapt their approach based on the specific goals and challenges of each project. By following a structured process, data scientists can effectively manage and leverage data to derive meaningful insights and make informed decisions.

The first step in the data science process is defining the problem statement and objectives. This involves clearly articulating the goals of the analysis, identifying the relevant stakeholders, and understanding the context in which the analysis will be conducted. By defining the problem statement upfront, data scientists can ensure that their analysis remains focused and aligned with the needs of the organization or project.

Once the problem statement has been defined, the next step is data collection and preparation. This involves gathering relevant data from various sources and formats, cleaning and preprocessing the data to remove errors and inconsistencies and transforming the data into a format suitable for analysis. Data collection and preparation are often the most time-consuming and labor-intensive steps in the data science process, but they are crucial for ensuring the quality and integrity of the data.

With the data prepared, the next step is exploratory data analysis (EDA), which involves visually exploring and summarizing the data to uncover patterns, trends, and relationships. EDA techniques include descriptive statistics, data visualization, and dimensionality reduction, which enable data scientists to gain insights into the underlying structure of the data. EDA helps data scientists identify outliers, detect patterns, and generate hypotheses for further analysis, laying the foundation for more advanced modeling techniques.

Following EDA, the next step is modeling, which involves building and evaluating predictive or descriptive models using statistical and machine learning techniques. This step may involve splitting the data into training and testing sets, selecting appropriate algorithms, tuning model parameters, and evaluating model performance using metrics such as accuracy, precision, recall, and F1-score. The goal of modeling is to develop a model that accurately captures the underlying patterns in the data and can be used to make predictions or generate insights.

Once a model has been developed, the next step is interpretation and evaluation, which involves interpreting the results of the analysis and evaluating the implications for the problem at hand. This may involve visualizing model predictions, conducting sensitivity analyses, and assessing the robustness of the results. Interpretation and evaluation are critical for ensuring that the insights derived from the analysis are meaningful and actionable, and that any conclusions drawn are supported by the evidence.

Finally, the last step in the data science process is communication and deployment, which involves presenting the results of the analysis to stakeholders and deploying any actionable insights or recommendations. This may involve creating visualizations, dashboards, or reports to communicate the findings effectively, and working with stakeholders to develop strategies for implementing the insights into practice. Effective communication and deployment are essential for ensuring that the value of the analysis is realized and that the insights derived from the data science process have a positive impact on decision-making and organizational outcomes.

In conclusion, the data science process is a systematic approach to extracting insights and knowledge from data, encompassing a series of steps that guide the analysis and interpretation of data. By following a structured process, data scientists can effectively manage and leverage data to derive meaningful insights and make informed decisions. From defining the problem statement and objectives to communication and deployment, each step in the data science process plays a critical role in ensuring the success of data-driven projects and initiatives.

Applications in Various Industries

Data science and analytics have revolutionized various industries, driving innovation, improving efficiency, and unlocking new opportunities for growth and development. From healthcare and finance to marketing and manufacturing, the applications of data science are vast and diverse, with each industry leveraging data-driven insights to solve complex problems and drive strategic decision-making.

In the healthcare industry, data science has transformed patient care, diagnosis, and treatment. Healthcare providers are using data analytics to improve patient outcomes, reduce costs, and enhance the overall quality of care. Electronic health records (EHRs) and medical imaging data are being analyzed to identify patterns and trends, predict disease progression, and personalize treatment plans. Machine learning algorithms are being used to develop predictive models for early disease detection, patient monitoring, and risk stratification, enabling healthcare providers to intervene proactively and deliver more targeted and effective care.

In the finance industry, data science is revolutionizing how financial institutions manage risk, detect fraud, and optimize investment strategies. Banks and financial institutions are using data analytics to assess creditworthiness, detect suspicious transactions, and identify potential market opportunities. Machine learning algorithms are being employed to analyze vast amounts of financial data in real-time, enabling traders and investors to make more informed decisions and mitigate risks. Additionally, data science techniques such as predictive modeling and algorithmic trading are being used to optimize investment portfolios and maximize returns.

In the marketing industry, data science is reshaping how businesses understand and engage with their customers. Marketing campaigns are becoming increasingly data-driven, with companies using customer segmentation, predictive modeling, and sentiment analysis to target their marketing efforts more effectively. Data analytics is being used to track consumer behavior, measure campaign performance, and optimize marketing strategies across various channels, including social media, email, and online advertising. Machine learning algorithms are being employed to personalize marketing messages and recommendations, delivering more relevant and engaging experiences to customers.

In the manufacturing industry, data science is driving improvements in efficiency, productivity, and product quality. Manufacturing companies are using data analytics to optimize production processes, reduce downtime, and minimize defects. Sensor data from production equipment is being analyzed in real-time to detect anomalies, predict equipment failures, and schedule maintenance proactively. Machine learning algorithms are being used to optimize supply chain management, forecast demand, and improve inventory management, ensuring that manufacturers can meet customer demands while minimizing costs and waste.

In the transportation industry, data science is revolutionizing how people and goods are moved from one place to another. Transportation companies are using data analytics to optimize route planning, reduce congestion, and improve safety. GPS data from vehicles and smartphones is being analyzed to optimize traffic flow, predict travel times, and identify areas of congestion. Machine learning algorithms are being employed to develop predictive models for vehicle maintenance, driver behavior, and accident prevention, enabling transportation companies to reduce costs and improve overall efficiency.

In conclusion, data science and analytics have a wide range of applications across various industries, from healthcare and finance to marketing and manufacturing. By leveraging data-driven insights, organizations can drive innovation, improve efficiency, and make more informed decisions. Whether it's optimizing patient care, detecting fraud, targeting marketing campaigns, or improving production processes, the potential for data science to transform industries is virtually limitless. As the volume and complexity of data continue to grow, organizations that embrace data science and analytics will be better positioned to succeed in the increasingly competitive and data-driven world.

CHAPTER III

Understanding Data

Types of Data: Structured vs. Unstructured

In the realm of data science and analytics, data comes in various forms, each with its unique characteristics and challenges. Two primary types of data that are commonly encountered are structured and unstructured data. Understanding the differences between these types of data is essential for effectively managing and analyzing data to derive meaningful insights and make informed decisions.

Structured data refers to data that is organized in a predefined format, typically stored in tables with rows and columns. This format allows for easy storage, retrieval, and analysis using traditional database management systems. Examples of structured data include spreadsheets, relational databases, and CSV files. Structured data is characterized by its consistency and predictability, making it relatively straightforward to process and analyze. Common operations performed on structured data include querying, filtering, and aggregating, using SQL or other database query languages. Structured data is prevalent in business applications, where it is used for tasks such as transaction processing, inventory management, and financial reporting.

On the other hand, unstructured data refers to data that does not have a predefined structure and is often stored in its raw or natural form. Unstructured data can take many different forms, including text, images, videos, audio files, and social media posts. Unlike structured data, unstructured data does not fit neatly into rows and columns and may contain a mix of text, images, and other media types. This lack of structure makes unstructured data more challenging to process and analyze, as it requires specialized techniques and tools to extract insights effectively. Common techniques used to analyze unstructured data include natural language processing (NLP), computer vision, and audio analysis. Unstructured data is prevalent in sources such as social media, email communications, and sensor data, where it is used for tasks such as sentiment analysis, image recognition, and speech recognition.

While structured and unstructured data have distinct characteristics, they are not mutually exclusive, and many datasets contain a combination of both structured and unstructured data. This hybrid data landscape presents both opportunities and challenges for data scientists, who must develop strategies for effectively managing and analyzing diverse data types. One approach is to use data integration techniques to combine structured and unstructured data into a unified dataset, allowing for more comprehensive analysis and insights. Another approach is to use advanced analytics techniques, such as machine learning and deep learning, to extract insights from unstructured data and integrate them with structured data for a more holistic understanding of the underlying phenomena.

The rise of big data technologies and platforms has further blurred the distinction between structured and unstructured data, as organizations increasingly collect and analyze vast amounts of data from diverse sources. Technologies such as Hadoop, Spark, and NoSQL databases have enabled organizations to store and process massive volumes of both structured and unstructured data in a distributed and scalable manner. Additionally, advances in artificial intelligence and machine learning have opened up new possibilities for analyzing unstructured data, allowing organizations to uncover hidden patterns and insights that were previously inaccessible.

In conclusion, structured and unstructured data represent two primary types of data that are encountered in data science and analytics. While structured data is organized in a predefined format and is relatively easy to process and analyze, unstructured data lacks a predefined structure and presents unique challenges for analysis. However, both types of data offer valuable insights and opportunities for organizations looking to leverage data to drive innovation, improve decision-making, and gain a competitive edge in today's data-driven world. By understanding the characteristics of structured and unstructured data and developing strategies for effectively managing and analyzing diverse data types, organizations can unlock the full potential of their data assets and derive actionable insights that drive business success.

Data Sources and Collection Methods

Data is the lifeblood of data science and analytics, serving as the raw material from which insights and knowledge are derived. In the modern world, data is generated at an unprecedented rate and from a multitude of sources, ranging from traditional databases to social media platforms and Internet of Things (IoT) devices. Understanding the various data sources and collection methods is essential for data scientists to effectively gather, manage, and analyze data to extract meaningful insights and make informed decisions.

One of the primary sources of data is internal data, which includes data generated within an organization's own systems and processes. This may include transactional data from enterprise resource planning (ERP) systems, customer data from customer relationship management

(CRM) systems, and operational data from manufacturing or supply chain management systems. Internal data sources provide valuable insights into an organization's operations, performance, and customer interactions, making them a rich source of information for data-driven decision-making.

Another important source of data is external data, which includes data obtained from outside sources such as third-party vendors, government agencies, and public datasets. External data sources may include demographic data, economic indicators, weather data, and industry reports, among others. External data sources can provide valuable context and insights that complement internal data, enabling organizations to gain a more comprehensive understanding of market trends, consumer behavior, and competitive dynamics.

In addition to internal and external data sources, data can also be collected from sensor networks, IoT devices, and other connected devices. These devices generate vast amounts of data in real-time, capturing information about environmental conditions, machine performance, and user interactions. Sensor data can be used for a wide range of applications, including predictive maintenance, environmental monitoring, and smart city initiatives. By collecting and analyzing sensor data, organizations can identify patterns, detect anomalies, and optimize operations in real-time, leading to improved efficiency and performance.

The methods used to collect data vary depending on the type of data and the specific requirements of the project. Traditional methods of data collection include surveys, interviews, and observation, which are used to gather qualitative and quantitative data from human participants. Surveys and interviews are commonly used in market research, social science research, and customer feedback collection, while observation is often used in ethnographic studies and usability testing.

In addition to traditional methods, data can also be collected passively through digital channels such as websites, mobile apps, and social media platforms. Web analytics tools track user interactions on websites and mobile apps, providing insights into user behavior, preferences, and engagement metrics. Social media monitoring tools analyze conversations and sentiment on social media platforms, enabling organizations to understand public opinion, detect emerging trends, and monitor brand perception.

Furthermore, data can be collected through automated processes such as web scraping, which involves extracting data from websites and online databases using software tools. Web scraping is commonly used for tasks such as competitive intelligence, price monitoring, and content aggregation. Similarly, data can be collected through APIs (Application Programming Interfaces), which allow developers to access and retrieve data from external sources such as social media platforms, weather APIs, and financial data providers.

In conclusion, data sources and collection methods play a crucial role in the data science and analytics process, providing the foundation upon which insights and knowledge are built. By understanding the various sources of data and the methods used to collect it, data scientists can effectively gather, manage, and analyze data to extract meaningful insights and make informed decisions. Whether it's internal data from organizational systems, external data from third-party sources, or sensor data from IoT devices, each data source offers unique opportunities for organizations to gain valuable insights and drive innovation in today's data-driven world.

Data Quality and Preprocessing

Data quality and preprocessing are critical steps in the data science and analytics process, as they lay the foundation for accurate and reliable analysis. Data quality refers to the degree to which data meets the requirements and expectations of its intended use, including aspects such as accuracy, completeness, consistency, and reliability. Poor data quality can lead to erroneous conclusions and biased insights, undermining the validity and credibility of the analysis. Therefore, ensuring data quality is essential for producing meaningful and actionable insights that drive informed decision-making.

Data preprocessing is the process of cleaning, transforming, and preparing raw data for analysis. This involves identifying and addressing issues such as missing values, outliers, inconsistencies, and noise that can affect the quality and reliability of the data. Common techniques used in data preprocessing include data cleaning, data imputation, feature scaling, and dimensionality reduction. Data cleaning involves identifying and correcting errors in the data, such as typos, duplicates, and formatting issues. Data imputation involves filling in missing values using techniques such as mean imputation, median imputation, or predictive modeling. Feature scaling involves standardizing or normalizing the scale of features to ensure that they have a consistent range and distribution. Dimensionality reduction involves reducing the number of features in the dataset to improve computational efficiency and reduce the risk of overfitting.

One of the main challenges in data quality and preprocessing is dealing with missing values, which can arise due to various reasons such as data entry errors, equipment failures, or non-response in surveys. Missing values can introduce bias and reduce the effectiveness of the analysis, so it is essential to handle them appropriately. Depending on the nature of the data and the extent of missingness, different techniques can be used to impute missing values. For example, mean imputation replaces missing values with the mean of the observed values for that feature, while median imputation replaces them with the median. More advanced techniques, such as predictive modeling or multiple imputation, can be used for cases where the missingness is more complex or systematic.

Another common challenge in data preprocessing is dealing with outliers, which are data points that deviate significantly from the rest of the dataset. Outliers can skew statistical measures and distort the results of analysis, so it is important to identify and handle them appropriately. Various techniques can be used to detect and remove outliers, such as visual inspection, statistical methods (e.g., z-score or interquartile range), or machine learning algorithms (e.g., isolation forest or k-nearest neighbors). The choice of technique depends on factors such as the distribution of the data and the specific requirements of the analysis.

In addition to missing values and outliers, data preprocessing also involves dealing with inconsistencies and noise in the data. Inconsistencies may arise due to discrepancies in data entry formats or coding conventions, while noise may result from measurement errors or random fluctuations in the data. Data cleaning techniques such as standardization, normalization, or data transformation can help address these issues and improve the overall quality of the data. Additionally, feature engineering techniques such as aggregation, binning, or encoding can be used to create new features or simplify existing ones, further enhancing the quality and usefulness of the data for analysis.

Overall, data quality and preprocessing are critical steps in the data science and analytics process, ensuring that the data used for analysis is accurate, reliable, and suitable for its intended purpose. By addressing issues such as missing values, outliers, inconsistencies, and noise, data scientists can improve the quality of the data and produce more robust and meaningful insights. Through careful data preprocessing, organizations can unlock the full potential of their data assets and derive actionable insights that drive innovation, improve decision-making, and create value in today's data-driven world.

CHAPTER IV

Statistical Foundations

Descriptive Statistics

Descriptive statistics is a branch of statistics that focuses on summarizing and describing the characteristics of a dataset. It provides a way to organize, visualize, and understand the patterns and trends present in the data, helping researchers and analysts gain insights into the underlying phenomena. Descriptive statistics encompasses a wide range of techniques and measures, each serving a specific purpose in summarizing different aspects of the data.

One of the most basic measures of descriptive statistics is the measures of central tendency, which describe the central or typical value of a dataset. The most common measures of central tendency include the mean, median, and mode. The mean, or average, is calculated by summing all the values in the dataset and dividing by the total number of values. The median is the middle value of the dataset when arranged in ascending order, while the mode is the most frequently occurring value. These measures provide information about the typical value or typical behavior of the data, helping to summarize the overall distribution.

In addition to measures of central tendency, descriptive statistics also include measures of variability or dispersion, which describe the spread or variability of the data around the central value. Common measures of variability include the range, variance, and standard deviation. The range is the difference between the maximum and minimum values in the dataset, providing a simple measure of spread. The variance measures the average squared deviation from the mean, while the standard deviation is the square root of the variance. These measures provide information about the extent to which the values in the dataset deviate from the central value, helping to characterize the variability or spread of the data.

Another important aspect of descriptive statistics is the visualization of data through graphical methods. Graphical methods such as histograms, box plots, and scatter plots provide visual representations of the distribution, shape, and relationships present in the data. Histograms display the frequency distribution of a continuous variable, while box plots summarize the distribution of a continuous variable and highlight outliers. Scatter plots are used to visualize the relationship between two continuous variables, showing how changes in one variable are associated with changes in the other. These graphical methods provide intuitive ways to explore and interpret the data, allowing researchers and analysts to identify patterns, trends, and outliers more easily.

Descriptive statistics also include measures of association or correlation, which describe the strength and direction of the relationship between two variables. The most common measure of correlation is the Pearson correlation coefficient, which ranges from -1 to +1 and indicates the strength and direction of the linear relationship between two variables. A correlation coefficient close to +1 indicates a strong positive correlation, while a correlation coefficient close to -1 indicates a strong negative correlation. A correlation coefficient close to 0 indicates little or no linear relationship between the variables. These measures provide information about the degree to which changes in one variable are associated with changes in another variable, helping to identify potential relationships or dependencies in the data.

Overall, descriptive statistics play a crucial role in summarizing and describing the characteristics of a dataset, providing valuable insights into the underlying patterns and trends. By calculating measures of central tendency, variability, and association, and visualizing the data through graphical methods, researchers and analysts can gain a deeper understanding of the data and identify key insights and relationships. Descriptive statistics provide a solid foundation for further analysis and interpretation, serving as the starting point for more advanced statistical techniques and modeling approaches. Whether exploring a new dataset or summarizing the findings of a research study, descriptive statistics are essential tools for making sense of data and communicating results effectively.

Inferential Statistics

Inferential statistics is a branch of statistics that involves making inferences or predictions about a population based on a sample of data drawn from that population. Unlike descriptive statistics, which focus on summarizing and describing the characteristics of a dataset, inferential statistics allow researchers and analysts to draw conclusions about the population as a whole, based on the characteristics of the sample. Inferential statistics play a crucial role in scientific research, business decision-making, and policy analysis, providing a way to generalize findings from a sample to the larger population.

One of the key concepts in inferential statistics is hypothesis testing, which involves testing a hypothesis or claim about a population parameter using sample data. Hypothesis testing typically involves two competing hypotheses: the null hypothesis (H0) and the alternative hypothesis (Ha). The null hypothesis represents the status quo or default assumption, while the alternative hypothesis represents the claim or assertion being tested.

Researchers use sample data to calculate a test statistic, such as a t-statistic or z-statistic, which is then compared to a critical value or p-value to determine whether to reject the null hypothesis in favor of the alternative hypothesis. If the test statistic falls within the critical region or if the p-value is less than a predetermined significance level (e.g., 0.05), the null hypothesis is rejected, and the alternative hypothesis is accepted.

Descriptive and Inferential Statistics

Another important concept in inferential statistics is confidence intervals, which provide a range of values within which the population parameter is likely to fall, based on the sample data. Confidence intervals are constructed using the sample mean and standard error of the mean, along with a specified confidence level (e.g., 95% confidence level). The width of the confidence interval reflects the precision of the estimate, with narrower intervals indicating greater precision. Confidence intervals allow researchers to quantify the uncertainty associated with their estimates and provide a range of plausible values for the population parameter, helping to communicate the reliability of the findings to stakeholders.

In addition to hypothesis testing and confidence intervals, inferential statistics also include techniques such as regression analysis, analysis of variance (ANOVA), and chi-square tests, which are used to analyze relationships and make predictions about variables in the population. Regression analysis is used to model the relationship between a dependent variable and one or more independent variables, allowing researchers to make predictions or identify factors that influence the outcome of interest. ANOVA is used to compare means across multiple groups or treatments, while chi-square tests are used to analyze categorical data and test for associations between variables.

One of the main challenges in inferential statistics is ensuring that the assumptions underlying the statistical tests and techniques are met. Violations of these assumptions can lead to biased estimates, incorrect conclusions, and invalid inferences. Common assumptions include normality, homogeneity of variance, independence of observations, and linearity of relationships. Researchers use diagnostic tests and graphical methods to assess whether these assumptions are met and to determine the appropriate statistical techniques for analyzing the data.

Overall, inferential statistics provide a powerful toolkit for drawing conclusions and making predictions about populations based on sample data. By testing hypotheses, constructing confidence intervals, and analyzing relationships between variables, researchers and analysts can gain insights into the underlying patterns and trends in the population, helping to inform decision-making and guide future research efforts. While inferential statistics come with their challenges and limitations, they remain a cornerstone of scientific inquiry and data-driven decision-making, allowing researchers to uncover new knowledge and drive innovation in a wide range of fields.

Probability Theory and Distributions

Probability theory is a fundamental branch of mathematics that deals with the study of uncertainty and randomness. It provides a framework for quantifying uncertainty and making predictions about the likelihood of different outcomes. In probability theory, events are assigned probabilities, which represent the likelihood of the event occurring. These probabilities range from 0 to 1, with 0 indicating impossibility and 1 indicating certainty. Probability theory is used in a wide range of fields, including statistics, economics, engineering, and physics, to model and analyze uncertain phenomena.

One of the key concepts in probability theory is the probability distribution, which describes the possible outcomes of a random variable and their associated probabilities. There are two main types of probability distributions: discrete distributions and continuous distributions. Discrete distributions describe random variables that can take on a finite or countable number of distinct values, such as the outcomes of rolling a die or the number of heads in a series of coin flips. Examples of discrete distributions include the uniform distribution, the binomial distribution, and the Poisson distribution. Continuous distributions, on the other hand, describe random variables that can take on any value within a certain range, such as the heights of individuals or the temperatures recorded on a thermometer. Examples of continuous distributions include the normal distribution, the exponential distribution, and the uniform distribution.

The normal distribution, also known as the Gaussian distribution, is perhaps the most well-known and widely used probability distribution. It is characterized by a symmetric, bell-shaped curve and is often used to model naturally occurring phenomena such as heights, weights, and test scores. The normal distribution is defined by two parameters: the mean, which represents the center of the distribution, and the standard deviation, which represents the spread or variability of the distribution. Many statistical techniques and methods assume of normality, making the normal distribution a key concept in probability theory and statistics.

Another important concept in probability theory is the central limit theorem, which states that the distribution of the sum or average of a large number of independent and identically distributed random variables approaches a normal distribution, regardless of the underlying distribution of the individual random variables. This theorem has wide-ranging implications for statistical inference and hypothesis testing, as it allows researchers to make inferences about population parameters based on sample data, even when the population distribution is unknown or non-normal.

In addition to the normal distribution, there are many other probability distributions that are commonly used in statistics and data analysis. The binomial distribution describes the number of successes in a fixed number of independent Bernoulli trials, such as the number of heads in a series of coin flips or the number of defective items in a batch of products. The Poisson distribution describes the number of events occurring in a fixed interval of time or space, such as the number of arrivals at a busy intersection or the number of phone calls received by a call center in a given hour. These distributions have specific properties and applications that make them useful for modeling and analyzing diverse types of data.

In conclusion, probability theory and distributions provide a powerful framework for modeling and analyzing uncertain phenomena. From discrete distributions that describe the outcomes of simple experiments to continuous distributions that model complex real-world phenomena, probability theory offers a rich toolkit for quantifying uncertainty and making predictions about the likelihood of different outcomes. By understanding the concepts of probability theory and probability distributions, researchers and analysts can gain insights into the underlying patterns and trends in their data, helping to inform decision-making and guide future research efforts in a wide range of fields.

CHAPTER V

Mathematics for Data Science

Linear Algebra

Linear algebra forms the backbone of mathematics for data science, providing essential tools and techniques for analyzing and manipulating data. In the context of data science, linear algebra is used to represent and process data in various forms, including vectors, matrices, and linear transformations. Understanding linear algebra is crucial for performing operations such as dimensionality reduction, feature extraction, and model optimization, which are fundamental to data analysis and machine learning.

At the heart of linear algebra are vectors, which represent quantities that have both magnitude and direction. In the context of data science, vectors are used to represent individual data points or observations, as well as features or attributes of the data. For example, in a dataset of student records, each student's grades in different subjects could be represented as a vector, with each grade corresponding to a component of the vector. Vectors can be combined using operations such as addition, scalar multiplication, and dot products, allowing for mathematical manipulation and analysis of the data.

Matrices are another fundamental concept in linear algebra that play a significant role in data science. Matrices are used to represent datasets, transformations, and relationships between variables in various applications. For instance, in a dataset of housing prices, each row of the matrix could represent a different house, with columns representing features such as size, location, and price. Matrices can be manipulated using operations such as addition, multiplication, and inversion, enabling transformations and analyses of the data. Matrix operations are used in machine learning algorithms such as linear regression, principal component analysis (PCA), and singular value decomposition (SVD), which are essential techniques for data analysis and modeling.

Linear transformations are mathematical functions that map vectors from one vector space to another while preserving certain properties such as linearity and proportionality. In data science, linear transformations are used to preprocess and transform data, as well as to model relationships between variables. For example, in image processing, linear transformations such as rotations, scalings, and translations are used to manipulate and enhance images. In machine learning, linear transformations are used to map input features to output predictions, enabling the construction of predictive models.

Eigenvalues and eigenvectors are key concepts in linear algebra that arise in the study of linear transformations and matrices. Eigenvalues represent scalar values that characterize the behavior of linear transformations, while eigenvectors represent the corresponding directions of transformation. In data science, eigenvalues and eigenvectors are used in techniques such as PCA and SVD to analyze and decompose datasets into their principal components or latent factors. These techniques are used for tasks such as dimensionality reduction, feature extraction, and data compression, allowing for more efficient and effective analyses of large and complex datasets.

In conclusion, linear algebra is a fundamental branch of mathematics that underpins many aspects of data science. From representing and manipulating data using vectors and matrices to analyzing and modeling relationships using linear transformations and eigenvalues, linear algebra provides essential tools and techniques for data analysis and machine learning. By understanding the concepts and applications of linear algebra, data scientists can gain insights into the structure and relationships within their data, enabling them to develop more accurate and efficient models and algorithms. Linear algebra serves as a cornerstone of mathematics for data science, empowering researchers and practitioners to unlock the potential of data and drive innovation in the field.

Calculus

Calculus serves as a foundational pillar of mathematics for data science, providing essential tools and concepts for understanding the behavior of functions and analyzing relationships between variables. In the realm of data science, calculus finds extensive applications in various areas such as optimization, modeling, and statistical analysis. One of the fundamental concepts of calculus is the derivative, which represents the rate of change of a function with respect to its input variable. Derivatives are pivotal in data science for analyzing the behavior of functions, identifying critical points such as maxima and minima, and optimizing functions to achieve specific objectives. For instance, derivatives are extensively used in gradient-based optimization algorithms like gradient descent, which lies at the heart of training machine learning models.

Integral calculus is another vital component of mathematics for data science. Integrals are employed to compute the accumulation of quantities over a continuous interval, representing areas under curves and the total mass or volume of objects. In data science, integrals are utilized in techniques such as probability density functions (PDFs) and cumulative distribution functions (CDFs) to model and analyze random variables. Moreover, integrals are integral (pun intended) to techniques like Bayesian inference, where they are employed to compute integrals over probability distributions, enabling researchers to make probabilistic inferences about the underlying phenomena.

Limits, a core concept in calculus, are utilized to comprehend the behavior of functions as the input variable approaches a particular value. In data science, limits play a crucial role in analyzing the convergence of iterative algorithms, such as gradient descent, and characterizing the behavior of functions at points of discontinuity or singularity. Understanding limits allows data scientists to make informed decisions about the stability and convergence properties of algorithms, contributing to the development of robust and efficient computational techniques.

Differential equations are mathematical equations that describe the relationships between variables and their rates of change. They find extensive applications in modeling dynamic systems and processes in diverse domains such as physics, engineering, and economics. In data science, differential equations are employed in techniques like time series analysis, where they are used to model and forecast the behavior of time-varying data. Differential equations also play a crucial role in stochastic processes and Markov chains, which are utilized to model and analyze random sequences of events in probabilistic systems.

Numerical methods, including finite difference methods, numerical integration, and numerical optimization, are computational techniques utilized to approximate solutions to mathematical problems that cannot be solved analytically. In data science, numerical methods are indispensable for computing derivatives, integrals, and solutions to differential equations, as well as for solving optimization problems and performing simulations. These techniques enable data scientists to analyze and model complex real-world phenomena, providing insights and solutions that drive innovation and decision-making in data-driven applications.

In summary, calculus forms an integral part of mathematics for data science, providing fundamental tools and techniques for understanding and analyzing mathematical functions and relationships. From derivatives and integrals to limits and differential equations, calculus plays a vital role in developing and optimizing algorithms, modeling dynamic systems, and making informed decisions in data-driven applications. By leveraging the concepts and methodologies of calculus, data scientists can extract valuable insights from data, develop accurate models, and drive innovation in diverse domains. Calculus serves as a cornerstone of mathematics for data science, empowering researchers and practitioners to unlock the full potential of data and make significant contributions to the field.

Optimization Techniques

Optimization techniques play a pivotal role in data science, offering essential tools and methodologies for finding the best solutions to complex mathematical problems and optimizing various aspects of data analysis and machine learning models. In the realm of data science, optimization techniques are utilized to train machine learning models, fine-tune hyperparameters, and solve optimization problems that arise in diverse applications. Understanding optimization techniques is crucial for developing efficient algorithms, designing effective experiments, and making informed decisions in data-driven applications.

Gradient descent is one of the most fundamental optimization techniques in data science. It is an iterative optimization algorithm used to minimize a loss function and find the optimal parameters of a model. In gradient descent, the gradient of the loss function with respect to the model parameters is computed, and the parameters are updated iteratively in the direction of the negative gradient to decrease the loss. By adjusting the parameters based on the gradient, gradient descent converges to a local minimum of the loss function, enabling the optimization of machine learning models such as linear regression, logistic regression, and neural networks.

Stochastic gradient descent (SGD) is a variant of gradient descent that is particularly useful in large-scale machine learning problems where the training dataset is too large to fit into memory. Instead of computing the gradient of the loss function using the entire dataset, SGD computes an approximate gradient using a randomly selected subset of the data, known as a mini-batch. By updating the parameters based on mini-batch gradients, SGD can converge to a solution more quickly and with less computational cost than traditional gradient descent, making it well-suited for training deep learning models and handling large-scale datasets.

In addition to gradient-based optimization techniques, there are also derivative-free optimization techniques that do not rely on the gradient of the loss function. These techniques include evolutionary algorithms, simulated annealing, and genetic algorithms, which use stochastic search methods to explore the parameter space and find optimal solutions. Derivative-free optimization techniques are particularly useful in optimization problems with non-smooth or discontinuous objective functions, as well as in situations where the gradient of the loss function is difficult or expensive to compute.

Convex optimization is another important class of optimization techniques in data science, dealing with optimization problems where the objective function and constraints are convex. Convex optimization problems have desirable properties such as a unique global minimum and efficient algorithms for finding the optimal solution. Convex optimization techniques are used in various machine learning algorithms such as support vector machines (SVMs), linear programming, and robust optimization, which are widely used in classification, regression, and optimization tasks in data science.

Bayesian optimization is a probabilistic optimization technique that is commonly used for hyperparameter tuning and model selection in machine learning. Bayesian optimization builds a probabilistic model of the objective function based on observed evaluations and uses this model to guide the search for optimal hyperparameters. By iteratively selecting hyperparameters to evaluate based on the probabilistic model, Bayesian optimization can efficiently explore the parameter space and find optimal solutions with a limited number of evaluations, making it particularly useful in situations where the objective function is expensive to evaluate.

In summary, optimization techniques are indispensable tools in data science for finding optimal solutions to complex mathematical problems and optimizing various aspects of data analysis and machine learning models. From gradient descent and stochastic gradient descent to derivative-free optimization and convex optimization, a wide range of techniques are available for solving optimization problems in data science. By understanding and leveraging these techniques effectively, data scientists can develop more accurate models, make better decisions, and extract valuable insights from data, leading to improved performance and outcomes in data-driven applications. Optimization techniques serve as a cornerstone of mathematics for data science, empowering researchers and practitioners to unlock the full potential of data and drive innovation in the field.

CHAPTER VI

Programming for Data Science

Introduction to Python and R

Python and R are two of the most popular programming languages in the realm of data science and statistical analysis. Both languages offer robust libraries and tools specifically designed for handling data, making them indispensable for data scientists, statisticians, and researchers alike. Python, known for its versatility and ease of use, has gained widespread adoption in the data science community due to its extensive ecosystem of libraries such as NumPy, pandas, and scikit-learn. These libraries provide powerful tools for data manipulation, analysis, and machine learning, allowing users to perform a wide range of tasks from data preprocessing to model deployment seamlessly.

On the other hand, R is renowned for its comprehensive statistical capabilities and rich visualization tools, making it a preferred choice for statisticians and researchers working with data. R's extensive collection of packages such as ggplot2, dplyr, and tidyr enable users to perform sophisticated statistical analyses and create compelling visualizations with ease. Moreover, R's interactive development environment (IDE), RStudio, provides a user-friendly interface for writing code, exploring data, and generating reports, making it an ideal platform for statistical analysis and reproducible research.

While Python and R have distinct strengths and specialties, they also share many similarities and can complement each other effectively in data science workflows. Both languages support a wide range of data types and structures, including vectors, matrices, data frames, and lists, making it easy to manipulate and analyze data regardless of its format. Additionally, both Python and R offer integration with other programming languages and tools, allowing users to leverage existing code and resources seamlessly in their data science projects.

Furthermore, Python and R are both open-source languages with active communities of developers and users contributing to their development and maintenance. This vibrant ecosystem ensures that users have access to a wealth of resources, tutorials, and documentation to support their learning and development efforts. Whether through online forums, user groups, or community-driven projects, Python and R users can collaborate, share knowledge, and solve problems collectively, fostering a spirit of innovation and collaboration within the data science community.

In recent years, there has been a growing trend towards using both Python and R together in data science projects, often referred to as "R and Python interoperability." This approach allows users to leverage the strengths of each language while mitigating their respective weaknesses, ultimately enhancing the efficiency and effectiveness of data science workflows. For example, users can perform data preprocessing and exploratory analysis in R, then switch to Python for model training and deployment, seamlessly integrating the two languages within a single workflow.

In conclusion, Python and R are powerful programming languages with distinct strengths and specialties in the realm of data science and statistical analysis. While Python is known for its versatility and ease of use, R excels in statistical analysis and visualization. By leveraging the strengths of both languages and promoting interoperability between them, data scientists and researchers can enhance their productivity, tackle complex problems more effectively, and unlock new insights from their data. Whether through Python's extensive libraries or R's rich statistical capabilities, both languages offer valuable tools and resources for anyone working with data in the modern era.

Essential Libraries (Pandas, NumPy, SciPy)

In the realm of data science and numerical computing, three libraries stand out as indispensable tools: Pandas, NumPy, and SciPy. Together, they provide a comprehensive suite of functionalities for data manipulation, numerical computing, and scientific computing, making them essential components of the toolkit for data scientists, researchers, and engineers.

NumPy, short for Numerical Python, serves as the foundation upon which many other numerical computing libraries are built. At its core, NumPy provides support for multidimensional arrays and matrices, along with a wide range of mathematical functions to operate on these arrays efficiently. NumPy's array operations are implemented in highly optimized C and Fortran code, making them significantly faster than equivalent operations in pure Python. This efficiency is crucial for handling large datasets and performing complex numerical computations in data science applications.

Pandas, built on top of NumPy, offers high-level data structures and tools for data manipulation and analysis in Python. Pandas' primary data structures, the Series and DataFrame, are designed to handle labeled and relational data, respectively, making them ideal for tasks such as data cleaning, exploration, and transformation. Pandas provides a plethora of functions and methods for indexing, slicing, filtering, grouping, and aggregating data, enabling users to perform complex data manipulations with ease. Additionally, Pandas seamlessly integrates with other libraries and tools in the Python ecosystem, making it a versatile and powerful tool for data analysis and manipulation.

SciPy, short for Scientific Python, extends NumPy's functionality by providing additional tools and algorithms for scientific computing. SciPy includes modules for optimization, interpolation, integration, linear algebra, signal processing, and more, making it a comprehensive library for scientific computing tasks. One of SciPy's standout features is its optimization module, which offers a wide range of optimization algorithms for solving nonlinear optimization problems, constrained optimization problems, and least squares fitting problems. SciPy's interpolation module provides functions for interpolating data points and constructing spline interpolants, while its integration module offers functions for numerical integration and solving ordinary differential equations. These capabilities make SciPy an invaluable resource for scientists, engineers, and researchers working in fields such as physics, biology, and engineering.

Together, Pandas, NumPy, and SciPy form a powerful trio of libraries that enable users to perform a wide range of data manipulation, numerical computing, and scientific computing tasks in Python. Whether it's cleaning and analyzing data, solving complex mathematical problems, or conducting scientific experiments, these libraries provide the essential building blocks and tools needed to tackle real-world challenges in data science and scientific computing. Moreover, their open-source nature and active communities of developers ensure that they continue to evolve and improve over time, staying at the forefront of innovation in the field of data science and numerical computing.

In conclusion, Pandas, NumPy, and SciPy are essential libraries in the Python ecosystem for data science, numerical computing, and scientific computing. NumPy provides support for multidimensional arrays and efficient numerical computations, Pandas offers high-level data structures and tools for data manipulation and analysis, and SciPy extends NumPy's functionality with additional tools and algorithms for scientific computing tasks. Together, these libraries provide a comprehensive suite of functionalities that enable users to tackle complex problems and extract valuable insights from their data, making them indispensable tools for data scientists, researchers, and engineers alike.

Writing Efficient and Clean Code

Writing efficient and clean code is essential for any software development project, including those in the realm of data science. Efficient code not only executes faster but also consumes fewer computational resources, making it more scalable and cost-effective. Moreover, clean code is easier to read, understand, and maintain, reducing the likelihood of errors and facilitating collaboration among team members. In the context of data science, where projects often involve complex data manipulations and analyses, writing efficient and clean code is particularly crucial for ensuring reproducibility, scalability, and maintainability.

One of the fundamental principles of writing efficient code is to optimize algorithms and data structures for performance. This involves selecting the most appropriate algorithms and data structures for the task at hand, considering factors such as time complexity, space complexity, and scalability. For example, when performing operations on large datasets, choosing efficient algorithms and data structures, such as hash tables or binary search trees, can significantly improve the performance of the code. Similarly, avoiding unnecessary nested loops and redundant computations can help reduce the computational complexity of the code, leading to faster execution times.

Another key aspect of writing efficient code is to minimize unnecessary I/O operations and memory usage. This involves optimizing file I/O operations, database queries, and memory allocations to minimize latency and maximize throughput. For example, when reading data from files or databases, batching I/O operations and using streaming techniques can help reduce overhead and improve efficiency. Similarly, managing memory efficiently, such as using data compression techniques or memory-mapped files, can help reduce memory usage and improve performance, especially when working with large datasets.

In addition to optimizing algorithms and minimizing I/O operations, writing clean code is equally important for ensuring readability, maintainability, and reproducibility. Clean code follows best practices and coding conventions, making it easy to read, understand, and modify by other developers. This involves using descriptive variable names, meaningful comments, and consistent formatting to convey the intent of the code clearly. Moreover, breaking down complex tasks into smaller, modular functions and classes can help improve code organization and facilitate code reuse and testing.

Furthermore, writing clean code involves adhering to principles such as Don't Repeat Yourself (DRY) and Single Responsibility Principle (SRP), which promote code reusability, modularity, and separation of concerns. By eliminating duplicate code and ensuring that each function or class has a single responsibility, clean code becomes easier to maintain, debug, and extend over time. Moreover, writing unit tests and documentation alongside the code can help ensure its correctness and reliability, enabling other developers to verify its behavior and make informed decisions about its usage.

In conclusion, writing efficient and clean code is essential for developing scalable, maintainable, and reproducible data science projects. By optimizing algorithms, minimizing I/O operations, and managing memory efficiently, developers can improve the performance and scalability of their code. Similarly, by following best practices, coding conventions, and design principles, developers can enhance the readability, maintainability, and reproducibility of their code. Ultimately, writing efficient and clean code not only improves the productivity and collaboration of developers but also ensures the reliability and quality of data science projects, leading to more impactful and valuable insights from data.

CHAPTER VII

Exploratory Data Analysis (EDA)

Data Visualization Techniques

Exploratory Data Analysis (EDA) is a crucial phase in the data science workflow, where analysts and data scientists explore and understand the structure, patterns, and relationships within the dataset. Data visualization techniques play a central role in EDA, enabling analysts to gain insights into the data quickly and intuitively. By visualizing the data in various ways, analysts can identify trends, outliers, correlations, and distributions, leading to hypotheses and insights that guide further analysis and decision-making.

One of the most common data visualization techniques used in EDA is the use of histograms and density plots to visualize the distribution of numerical variables. Histograms provide a graphical representation of the frequency distribution of a numerical variable by dividing the data into bins and counting the number of observations in each bin. Density plots, on the other hand, provide a smoothed estimate of the probability density function of the data, allowing analysts to visualize the underlying distribution more clearly. By visualizing the distribution of numerical variables, analysts can identify skewness, multimodality, and other patterns that may indicate interesting features or anomalies in the data.

Another popular technique for visualizing numerical variables is the use of scatter plots to visualize the relationship between two variables. Scatter plots display individual data points as points on a two-dimensional plane, with one variable plotted on the x-axis and the other variable plotted on the y-axis. By examining the patterns and trends in the scatter plot, analysts can identify correlations, clusters, and outliers in the data. Additionally, scatter plots can be enhanced with color, size, or shape encoding to visualize additional dimensions of the data, such as categorical variables or group membership.

For categorical variables, bar charts and pie charts are commonly used to visualize the frequency distribution of different categories within the variable. Bar charts display the frequency of each category as bars of varying heights, while pie charts represent the proportion of each category as slices of a pie. These visualization techniques are useful for identifying the most common categories, as well as any imbalances or disparities in the distribution of categories within the variable. Additionally, bar charts and pie charts can be combined with other visualization techniques, such as stacked bar charts or grouped bar charts, to visualize multiple categorical variables simultaneously.

In addition to visualizing individual variables, analysts often use heatmaps and correlation matrices to visualize the relationships between multiple variables. Heatmaps display the pairwise correlations between variables as a color-coded matrix, with brighter colors indicating stronger correlations and darker colors indicating weaker correlations. Correlation matrices provide a numerical summary of the correlations between variables, while heatmaps offer a visual representation that allows analysts to identify patterns and clusters in the data easily. By visualizing the relationships between multiple variables, analysts can identify clusters, trends, and dependencies that may indicate underlying structures or relationships within the data.

In summary, data visualization techniques are essential tools for exploratory data analysis, enabling analysts to gain insights into the structure, patterns, and relationships within the dataset. By visualizing numerical variables with histograms, density plots, and scatter plots, analysts can identify distributions, correlations, and outliers in the data. Similarly, visualizing categorical variables with bar charts and pie charts allows analysts to explore the frequency distribution of categories within the variable. Heatmaps and correlation matrices provide a visual representation of the relationships between multiple variables, helping analysts identify clusters, trends, and dependencies in the data. Overall, data visualization techniques facilitate the exploration and understanding of data, guiding further analysis and decision-making in the data science workflow.

Identifying Patterns and Trends

Identifying patterns and trends is critical to data analysis and interpretation, enabling analysts to uncover valuable insights and make informed decisions. Patterns refer to recurring structures or behaviors within the data, while trends represent systematic changes or movements over time. In data science, identifying patterns and trends involves applying various statistical and analytical techniques to detect and interpret underlying relationships and dynamics within the dataset.

One of the fundamental techniques for identifying patterns and trends is statistical analysis, which involves summarizing and analyzing the distribution, central tendency, and variability of the data. Descriptive statistics such as mean, median, mode, and standard deviation provide measures of central tendency and variability, allowing analysts to characterize the overall behavior of the data. Moreover, visualizing the data with histograms, box plots, and time series plots can reveal patterns and trends in the distribution and variability of the data over time or across different groups or categories.

Time series analysis is another powerful technique for identifying patterns and trends in sequential data, such as stock prices, weather data, or sales figures. It involves modeling and forecasting the behavior of a variable over time, using techniques such as moving averages, exponential smoothing, and autoregressive integrated moving average (ARIMA) models. By analyzing the autocorrelation and seasonality of the data, analysts can identify patterns and trends in the temporal dynamics of the variable, such as seasonality, trends, and cycles.

Machine learning algorithms, such as clustering and classification algorithms, can also be used to identify patterns and trends in the data. Clustering algorithms, such as k-means and hierarchical clustering, group similar data points together based on their characteristics, allowing analysts to identify natural clusters or segments within the data. Classification algorithms, such as decision trees and random forests, can classify data points into different categories or classes based on their features. This enables analysts to identify patterns and trends in the relationships between variables.

Furthermore, association rule mining and sequence analysis techniques can identify patterns and trends in transactional and sequential data, such as market basket or clickstream data. Association rule mining algorithms, such as Apriori and FP-growth, identify frequent item sets and association rules within transactional data, revealing patterns and trends in the co-occurrence of items or events. Sequence analysis techniques, such as sequential pattern mining and episode discovery, identify temporal patterns and trends in sequential data, such as the sequential ordering of events or activities.

In addition to statistical and analytical techniques, domain knowledge and expertise play a crucial role in identifying patterns and trends in the data. By combining domain knowledge with data analysis techniques, analysts can uncover meaningful patterns and trends that may not be apparent from the data alone. For example, in financial data analysis, domain knowledge of economic indicators and market trends can help analysts more effectively interpret patterns and trends in stock prices and trading volumes.

In conclusion, identifying patterns and trends is fundamental to data analysis and interpretation, enabling analysts to uncover valuable insights and make informed decisions. By applying statistical and analytical techniques, such as descriptive statistics, time series analysis, and machine learning algorithms, analysts can identify patterns and trends in the distribution, dynamics, and relationships within the data. Moreover, by leveraging domain knowledge and expertise, analysts can interpret patterns and trends in the context of the domain, gaining deeper insights and understanding of the underlying phenomena. Identifying patterns and trends is essential for extracting actionable insights and driving meaningful outcomes in the data science workflow.

Hypothesis Testing

A primary statistical method for concluding population parameters from sample data is hypothesis testing. It entails developing a population parameter hypothesis, gathering sample data, and evaluating the strength of evidence opposing the null hypothesis using statistical techniques. Generally speaking, the alternative hypothesis (Ha) indicates the presence of an effect or a difference, whereas the null hypothesis (H0) represents the status quo or the absence of an impact. Finding sufficient evidence to support the alternative hypothesis and reject the null hypothesis is the aim of hypothesis testing.

One of the most used kinds of hypothesis testing is the t-test to compare the means of two independent samples. The t-statistic, which gauges the variation in sample means about sample variability, is computed by the t-test. Analysts can ascertain if the difference between the sample means is statistically significant by comparing the t-statistic to a critical value from the t-distribution or by computing the p-value associated with the t-statistic.

The chi-square test, which evaluates the independence of categorical variables in a contingency table, is another popular method for evaluating hypotheses. The chi-square statistic, which gauges the difference between the actual and predicted frequencies of the category variables, is computed by the chi-square test. Analysts can ascertain whether the categorical variables are independent or whether there is a statistically significant association between them by computing the p-value associated with the chi-square statistic or by comparing the chi-square statistic to a critical value from the chi-square distribution.

For various kinds of data and research problems, numerous alternative hypothesis testing methods are available, in addition to the t-test and chi-square test. Regression analysis, on the other hand, is used to evaluate the connection between a dependent variable and one or more independent variables. In contrast, analysis of variance (ANOVA) is used to compare the means of different independent groups. Analysts must select the best hypothesis testing technique depending on the type of data and the research topic. Each method has its assumptions, requirements, and limitations.

Analysts must consider the test's power and significance level (alpha) when conducting hypothesis testing. The test's power represents the likelihood of accurately rejecting the null hypothesis when it is untrue, whereas the significance level is usually set at 0.05 or 0.01 as the threshold for rejection. Analysts can balance the risk of Type I mistakes (false positives) and Type II errors (false negatives) and guarantee the validity and reliability of their hypothesis testing results by modifying the significance level and doing power assessments.

In conclusion, hypothesis testing is an effective statistical method for concluding population parameters from sample data. Analysts can evaluate the strength of evidence against the null hypothesis and decide whether an effect is there or absent by developing null and alternative hypotheses, gathering sample data, and applying the proper statistical techniques. Analysts can test research hypotheses rigorously and derive reliable conclusions from their data by employing hypothesis-testing techniques, such as regression analysis, chi-square testing, ANOVA, or t-testing.

CHAPTER VIII

Supervised Learning

Regression Analysis

Regression analysis is a statistical method for modeling and analyzing the connection between one or more independent variables and a dependent variable. It is frequently used to explain the causal links between variables, generate predictions, and guide decision-making in various sectors, including economics, finance, marketing, and social sciences. The linear equation $y = \beta 0 + \beta 1 x1 + \beta 2 x2 + \ldots + \varepsilon$ is commonly used in regression analysis to model the relationship between the independent and dependent variables. In this equation, y denotes the dependent variable, $x1$, $x2$, etc., the independent variables, $\beta 0$, $\beta 1$, $\beta 2$, etc., the regression coefficients, and ε denotes the error term. Estimating the regression coefficients that most closely match the observed data and generating dependent variable predictions from the values of the independent variables are the two main objectives of regression analysis.

Simple linear regression, which models the relationship between a single independent variable and a dependent variable, is one of the most used forms of regression analysis. Simple linear regression uses a straight line to represent the relationship between the independent and dependent variables, and least squares estimation is used to estimate the regression coefficients. Analysts can calculate the slope and intercept of the line and evaluate the strength and direction of the link between the variables by fitting a line to the observed data points and minimizing the sum of the squared differences between the observed and expected values.

By modeling the link between several independent variables and a dependent variable, multiple linear regression expands on the ideas of basic linear regression. A linear equation with multiple regression coefficients is used to model the relationship between the independent and dependent variables in multiple linear regression. Analysts can determine which independent variables have a statistically significant impact on the dependent variable and measure the strength and direction of those relationships by estimating the regression coefficients using least squares estimation and evaluating their significance using hypothesis testing techniques.

For various kinds of data and research problems, numerous other kinds of regression analysis techniques are accessible in addition to primary and multiple linear regression. For instance, polynomial regression uses polynomial functions to model nonlinear interactions between variables. In contrast, logistic regression models the relationship between one or more independent factors and a binary dependent variable. To address multicollinearity and overfitting problems in multiple regression models, further regression analysis approaches include ridge regression, lasso regression, and elastic net regression.

Numerous advantages and uses for regression analysis in data analysis and decision-making are available. It allows analysts to measure the correlations between variables, forecast future events, and pinpoint the variables that affect the dependent variable. Regression analysis is commonly used in marketing to estimate sales and customer behavior, in finance to predict stock prices and investment returns, and in healthcare to model illness risk factors and treatment outcomes. Regression analysis is also helpful for testing theories on the causal links between variables and informing interventions and policy choices across various disciplines.

To sum up, regression analysis is a potent statistical method that can be used to model and examine the relationship between variables, generate forecasts, and guide choices. Using regression analysis techniques such as logistic regression, multiple linear regression, or basic linear regression, analysts can quantify the correlations between variables, forecast future events, and pinpoint the factors that affect the dependent variable. Regression analysis is a popular tool used in many disciplines to promote innovation and advancement, make educated selections, and comprehend complex relationships.

Classification Algorithms

Based on previous observations, classification algorithms are a class of machine learning approaches that anticipate the categorical class labels of new examples. They are extensively used to categorize data into distinct groups and make defensible conclusions in various industries, such as image recognition, marketing, finance, and healthcare. Classification algorithms categorize new data points into established classes or categories by leveraging patterns and correlations found in the training data.

Logistic regression is a widely used approach for classifying data, which models the likelihood of a given instance falling into a specific class. Using a logistic function, logistic regression models the link between the independent factors and the dependent variable's log odds. Analysts can categorize events into binary classes according to their expected probability by setting a threshold, say 0.5, and utilizing maximum likelihood estimation to estimate the coefficients of the logistic function.

Another well-liked classification approach is decision trees, which divide the feature space into regions using a structure like a tree, with each leaf node denoting a class label. Decision trees use criteria like information gain or Gini impurity to calculate the optimal splits, recursively splitting the feature space into subsets based on the values of the independent variables. Analysts can categorize instances into classes based on the majority class in the relevant leaf node by moving through the decision tree from the root node to the leaf nodes.

Random forests, an ensemble learning technique, combine multiple decision trees to increase the robustness and accuracy of classification models. They construct numerous decision trees by employing bootstrapped samples of the training data and randomly choosing a subset of characteristics at each split. Random forests are among the most potent and extensively used classification algorithms today because they decrease overfitting and enhance generalization performance by combining the predictions of several decision trees.

Another practical classification approach is supporting vector machines (SVMs), which operate by determining the ideal hyperplane to divide the classes in the feature space. By identifying the decision boundary that maximizes the margin between the nearest data points of various courses, support vector machines (SVMs) optimize the margin between the classes. SVMs may identify cases with intricate feature correlations and learn nonlinear decision boundaries by mapping the data into higher-dimensional spaces using kernel functions.

In recent years, neural networks—intense learning models—have become the cutting edge of classification algorithms, demonstrating exceptional performance in various applications, including speech recognition, image recognition, and natural language processing. Multiple layers of interconnected neurons make up deep learning models, which can recognize complex patterns and correlations in high-dimensional data by learning hierarchical representations of the incoming data. Using neural networks trained on massive datasets with millions of parameters, analysts can create robust and highly accurate classification models that can handle a wide range of complicated and varied data types.

Apart from the well-known classification algorithms, several more approaches are accessible for diverse data kinds and study inquiries, including k-nearest neighbors (KNN), naive Bayes, and gradient boosting machines (GBM). Every classification algorithm has advantages, disadvantages, and underlying assumptions. Analysts must select the best method depending on the data type they are analyzing and their objectives. Analysts can drive innovation and advancement across a wide range of domains by utilizing the power of classification algorithms to categorize data into discrete categories, predict future outcomes, and extract valuable insights from their data.

Model Evaluation and Validation

In the machine learning workflow, model assessment and validation are essential steps that guarantee the trained models work well in real-world scenarios and effectively generalize to new data. While model validation entails verifying the model's performance using separate datasets or cross-validation methods, model evaluation evaluates a trained model's performance on a dataset. To help analysts make well-informed judgments about model selection, optimization, and deployment, model assessment and validation aim to quantify the model's correctness, reliability, and generalization capabilities.

Accuracy is a frequently employed metric in model evaluation, as it quantifies the percentage of properly classified cases in the dataset relative to all instances. Accuracy is a straightforward and understandable indicator of model performance. Still, it might not be appropriate for unbalanced datasets or disproportionately high prevalence of one class over the others. Other metrics, such as precision, recall, and F1-score, may be more useful in certain situations since they offer a more impartial evaluation of the model's performance across several classes.

Recall indicates the percentage of actual positive instances among all instances in the dataset that belong to the positive class. In contrast, precision is the percentage of genuine positive instances among all the cases the model predicted to be positive. The F1-score, the harmonic mean of the two, is a single metric that balances precision and recall. By taking both precision and recall into account, analysts can assess a model's performance more thoroughly and decide on model selection and optimization.

Area under the ROC curve (AUC-ROC) for binary classification models, mean squared error (MSE) for regression models, mean average precision (MAP) for information retrieval and ranking tasks, and many more evaluation metrics are available in addition to these binary classification metrics for various types of models and functions. Analysts must select the best assessment metric depending on the work at hand and the analysis's objectives. Each assessment metric has advantages, disadvantages, and interpretations.

Model validation techniques like cross-validation are employed when evaluating a trained model's generalization performance on separate datasets or subsets of the training data. In cross-validation, the dataset is divided into several folds, the model is trained on a subset of the data, and its performance is assessed on the remaining fold or folds. By repeating this process several times with different data partitions, analysts can acquire more accurate estimations of the model's performance and pinpoint potential sources of bias or variability in the evaluation findings.

Additionally, determining how resilient the model is to alterations in the data—such as shifts in the distribution or caliber of the input features—is another aspect of model assessment and validation. Robustness testing and sensitivity analysis techniques are used to assess the model's performance in various scenarios and spot any possible flaws or vulnerabilities. Analysts can evaluate the model's ability to withstand uncertainty and make well-informed judgments regarding its dependability and durability in practical situations through systematic manipulation of the input characteristics, disruption of the training data, or introduction of noise.

To sum up, the machine learning pipeline requires both model assessment and validation to ensure that learned models work well in real-world situations and generalize well to new data. Analysts can assess a model's accuracy, dependability, and capacity for generalization by measuring its performance using suitable metrics and validation methodologies. This allows analysts to make well-informed judgments regarding the model's selection, optimization, and implementation. Furthermore, analysts can find potential flaws or vulnerabilities and improve the model's dependability and resilience in various demanding situations by evaluating the model's robustness to variations in the data, performing sensitivity analyses, and performing robustness tests.

CHAPTER IX

Unsupervised Learning

Clustering Techniques

Unsupervised learning is a branch of machine learning that deals with unlabeled data. The goal is to discover patterns, structures, and relationships within the data without explicit supervision. Clustering techniques are a fundamental aspect of unsupervised learning. They aim to partition data points into groups or clusters based on their similarities or distances in the feature space. Clustering techniques are widely used in various applications, including customer segmentation, image segmentation, anomaly detection, and recommendation systems, to uncover hidden structures and insights in the data.

One of the most popular clustering algorithms is K-means clustering, which partitions data points into K clusters by iteratively assigning each data point to the nearest cluster centroid and updating the centroids based on the mean of the data points assigned to each cluster. K-means clustering aims to minimize the within-cluster sum of squares, effectively finding compact and well-separated clusters in the feature space. Analysts can identify the optimal clustering solution that best fits the data by specifying the number of clusters K and running the algorithm multiple times with different initializations.

Another widely used clustering algorithm is hierarchical clustering, which builds a hierarchy of clusters by recursively merging or splitting clusters based on their similarities or distances. Hierarchical clustering can be agglomerative, where each data point starts in its cluster and clusters are successively merged based on their pairwise distances, or divisive, where all data points begin in a single cluster and are successively split into smaller clusters. By visualizing the dendrogram produced by hierarchical clustering, analysts can explore the hierarchical structure of the data and determine the appropriate number of clusters based on their domain knowledge and objectives.

Density-based clustering algorithms, such as DBSCAN (Density-Based Spatial Clustering of Applications with Noise), identify clusters based on regions of high density separated by regions of low density in the feature space. DBSCAN classifies data points as core points, border points, or noise points based on their density and spatial proximity to other points, allowing it to discover clusters of arbitrary shapes and sizes. By specifying parameters such as the minimum number of points in a cluster and the maximum distance between points, analysts can control the granularity and density of the clusters identified by DBSCAN.

Other clustering techniques include Gaussian mixture models (GMMs), spectral clustering, and affinity propagation, each with strengths, weaknesses, and assumptions. GMMs model the data as a mixture of Gaussian distributions and estimate the parameters of the distributions using maximum likelihood estimation or expectation-maximization (EM) algorithms. Spectral clustering projects the data into a lower-dimensional space using spectral techniques and then applies K-means clustering or other partitioning algorithms to the projected data. Affinity propagation identifies exemplar data points representing the cluster centroids and assigns each data point to the nearest exemplar based on their similarities.

In addition to these clustering techniques, many other advanced algorithms and methods are available for clustering data, such as self-organizing maps (SOMs), hierarchical mixture models, and deep clustering methods. Each clustering technique has its strengths, weaknesses, and assumptions, and analysts must choose the appropriate technique based on the nature of the data, the desired cluster structure, and the goals of the analysis. By leveraging clustering techniques, analysts can uncover hidden structures and insights in the data, segmenting it into meaningful groups or clusters and informing decision-making and action in various domains.

Dimensionality Reduction

Dimension reduction, a fundamental technique in machine learning and data analysis, aims to reduce the number of features or dimensions in a dataset while maintaining its key attributes and structures. Numerous characteristics in high-dimensional datasets present several difficulties, such as overfitting, increased processing complexity, and limitations with visualization and interpretation. To overcome these difficulties, dimensionality reduction approaches convert the data into a lower-dimensional space while preserving as much pertinent information as possible.

One of the most popular dimensionality reduction methods is principal component analysis (PCA), which looks for a set of orthogonal axes known as principle components that capture the most significant variation in the data. PCA reduces the dimensionality of the dataset by locating the directions of maximum variation in the data and projecting the data onto these principle components. Analysts can achieve significant dimensionality reduction while maintaining the majority of the dataset's information by keeping only the top k principal components that account for the majority of the variance in the data.

The goal of t-distributed Stochastic Neighbor Embedding (t-SNE), another well-liked dimensionality reduction method, is to maintain the local and global structures of the data in a lower-dimensional environment. By minimizing the Kullback-Leibler divergence between the two distributions, t-SNE creates a probability distribution over pairs of data points in the high-dimensional space and a corresponding probability distribution in the low-dimensional space. The t-SNE method creates a low-dimensional data representation while maintaining its underlying structures and relationships. It maximizes a cost function that gauges the similarity between data points in the original and reduced domains.

One dimensionality reduction method that is especially helpful for supervised classification applications is linear discriminant analysis (LDA). Logistic regression analysis (LDA) aims to find the linear feature combinations that maximize between-class variation and minimize within-class variance. LDA lowers the dataset's dimensionality while maintaining its discriminative information by projecting the data onto the discriminant axes that maximize the separability between classes. LDA is frequently employed in applications where feature extraction and dimensionality reduction are essential for classification performance, such as speech recognition, face recognition, and bioinformatics.

Another dimensionality reduction method that is especially helpful for data having non-negative values, such as text or image data, is non-negative matrix factorization (NMF). The basis vectors and coefficients of the data in the reduced space are represented by two low-rank matrices created when NMF factorizes the data matrix. NMF finds a set of basis vectors that capture the underlying patterns and structures in the data by minimizing the reconstruction error between the original data and its low-rank approximation. This effectively reduces the dimensionality of the dataset while maintaining its non-negativity constraints.

Neural network topologies known as autoencoders are utilized for dimensionality reduction and unsupervised learning. An encoder network maps the input data to a lower-dimensional latent space, while a decoder network uses the latent space representation to reconstruct the original data. This is how autoencoders function. Analysts can learn a concise and helpful representation of the data in the latent space, thereby lowering its dimensionality while keeping its essential properties and structures, by training the autoencoder to minimize the reconstruction error between the input and output data. Apart from these widely used dimensionality reduction strategies, numerous more techniques and algorithms exist for various data and tasks, including Kernel PCA, Laplacian Eigenmaps, and Independent Component Analysis (ICA). Analysts must select the best dimensionality reduction technique depending on the type of data, the desired degree of reduction, and the analysis's objectives. Each dimensionality reduction technique has advantages, disadvantages, and underlying assumptions. Analysts can extract valuable knowledge and insights from high-dimensional datasets by utilizing dimensionality reduction techniques to lower computational complexity, improve interpretability, and optimize machine learning models and data analysis pipeline performance.

Anomaly Detection

In data analysis and machine learning, anomaly detection, sometimes called outlier detection, is a crucial activity that seeks to find data points or patterns that substantially vary from the norm or expected behavior. Anomalies can be caused by several things, such as fraudulent activity, malfunctioning sensors, mistakes made during data collecting, or unusual occurrences. Maintaining data quality, protecting the integrity of systems and processes, and averting any risks and dangers depend on detecting abnormalities. Generally speaking, there are three anomaly detection techniques: semi-supervised, unsupervised, and supervised. Each has advantages and disadvantages.

When an algorithm is trained on a labeled dataset that includes standard and abnormal examples, it can learn the traits and patterns of anomalies from the labeled data. This process is known as supervised anomaly identification. Support vector machines (SVMs), decision trees, and ensemble methods are examples of classification algorithms used in supervised anomaly detection techniques. These algorithms are trained to differentiate between normal and abnormal cases based on their attributes. Analysts can determine if the model can reliably and accurately detect anomalies by training it on labeled data and assessing its performance on an independent test set.

Conversely, unsupervised anomaly detection looks for anomalies purely through the inherent characteristics of the data; it does not require labeled data. Examples of unsupervised anomaly detection techniques are statistical techniques that find data points or regions that significantly differ from the rest of the data, such as distance-based algorithms, density estimates, and clustering. Methods based on clustering, including DBSCAN and k-means clustering, combine related data points into groups and identify non-clustered data points as anomalies. Density-based techniques that detect anomalies based on variations in the local density of data points include the Local Outlier Factor (LOF) and Isolation Forest. Anomalies are identified using distance-based techniques like Mahala Nobis distance and k-nearest neighbors (KNN), which consider the distances between the anomalies and nearby data points.

Semi-supervised anomaly detection combines aspects of supervised and unsupervised algorithms to find anomalies more successfully by utilizing a smaller amount of labeled data and a more significant amount of unlabeled data. Using both labeled and unlabeled data, semi-supervised techniques like self-training, co-training, and active learning iteratively improve the model's predictions. Analysts can increase the model's precision and efficiency in identifying anomalies by training it on a small, labeled dataset and then updating the model's parameters using more unlabeled data.

Apart from the conventional methods of anomaly detection, other sophisticated approaches and algorithms can be employed to identify irregularities in diverse kinds of data, including time series, spatial, and network data. Deep learning techniques like autoencoders and recurrent neural networks (RNNs) have demonstrated encouraging results in anomaly detection tasks by learning hierarchical representations of the data and identifying intricate patterns and relationships. In complex and dynamic contexts, anomaly detection models are also made more robust and reliable by using ensemble approaches, meta-learning techniques, and Bayesian approaches.

Anomaly detection, in general, is a crucial activity in machine learning and data analysis, allowing analysts to recognize and address possible dangers and vulnerabilities in systems and data. Analysts may effectively and efficiently identify abnormalities in complex datasets using supervised, unsupervised, and semi-supervised methodologies. This helps guarantee data and systems' integrity, dependability, and security. Creating and applying efficient anomaly detection methods will continue to be a vital area of study and innovation in data science and machine learning as data volumes rise and threats grow more complex.

CHAPTER X

Advanced Machine Learning

Ensemble Methods

Advanced machine learning techniques often involve ensemble methods, which combine multiple individual models to improve predictive performance and robustness. Ensemble methods harness the wisdom of crowds by aggregating the predictions of diverse models, leveraging their complementary strengths, and mitigating their weaknesses. One of the most popular ensemble methods is bagging, which stands for bootstrap aggregation. Bagging involves training multiple base models, such as decision trees or neural networks, on random subsets of the training data with replacement and aggregating their predictions through averaging or voting. By reducing the variance of individual models and improving generalization performance, bagging produces more robust and stable predictions, particularly in high-variance models prone to overfitting.

Another widely used ensemble method is boosting, which aims to sequentially improve the performance of weak learners by focusing on instances that previous models misclassify. AdaBoost (Adaptive Boosting) is one of the most popular boosting algorithms, which assigns higher weights to misclassified instances and trains subsequent models to focus on correcting these errors. AdaBoost produces a strong learner capable of capturing complex patterns and relationships in the data by combining the predictions of weak learners and adjusting their weights based on their performance.

Random forests are a powerful ensemble learning technique that combines bagging and feature randomness to build a collection of decision trees with high predictive accuracy and robustness. Random forests train multiple decision trees on random subsets of the training data and random subsets of the features, reducing the correlation between individual trees and promoting diversity in the ensemble. By aggregating the predictions of multiple decision trees through averaging or voting, random forests produce accurate and stable predictions, capable of handling high-dimensional data and capturing complex interactions between features.

Gradient boosting machines (GBMs) are another ensemble learning technique that sequentially builds a collection of weak learners, typically decision trees, to minimize a loss function. GBMs iteratively fit the weak learners to the residuals of the previous models, gradually reducing the error and improving the predictive performance of the ensemble. XGBoost (Extreme Gradient Boosting) and LightGBM are popular implementations of gradient boosting machines. They are known for their efficiency, scalability, and state-of-the-art performance in various machine-learning competitions and real-world applications.

Stacking, also known as stacked generalization, is a meta-ensemble method that combines the predictions of multiple base models using a higher-level model called a meta-learner or blender. Stacking involves training diverse base models on the training data and using their predictions as input features to train the meta-learner. By learning to combine the predictions of the base models, the meta-learner produces a final ensemble model capable of capturing the strengths of individual models and achieving superior predictive performance.

Ensemble methods offer several benefits over single models, including improved predictive accuracy, robustness, and interpretability. By combining the predictions of diverse models, ensemble methods mitigate the risk of overfitting and reduce the variance of individual models, producing more reliable and stable predictions. Moreover, ensemble methods provide insights into the underlying patterns and relationships in the data by aggregating the predictions of multiple models, enabling analysts to make informed decisions and extract valuable insights from complex and heterogeneous datasets. As machine learning advances, ensemble methods will remain a cornerstone of the field, driving innovation and progress in predictive modeling and data analysis.

Neural Networks and Deep Learning

Inspired by the architecture and operation of the human brain, neural networks, and deep learning constitute a state-of-the-art field in machine learning. These methods have allowed computers to understand intricate patterns and correlations from massive amounts of data, revolutionizing several industries like speech recognition, computer vision, and natural language processing. Layers of interconnected nodes, known as neurons, make up neural networks. Each layer is in charge of processing and modifying the input data. Neural networks with several hidden layers are called deep learning neural networks because they can learn hierarchical representations of the data and identify complex patterns and characteristics.

One of their main advantages is the capacity of neural networks and deep learning to automatically extract features and representations from unprocessed data, doing away with the need for labor-intensive feature engineering and preprocessing. Using shared weights and local connection, Convolutional Neural Networks (CNNs) is a deep neural network that excels at image identification tasks by extracting spatial hierarchies of features from images. CNNs may learn hierarchical representations of visual characteristics and perform state-of-the-art tasks like object identification, picture classification, and image segmentation by stacking numerous convolutional layers with pooling and activation functions.

Another deep neural network intended to handle sequential data is the recurrent neural network (RNN), which can process text, audio, and time series data. Because RNNs include recurrent connections, they can model complicated sequences and produce predictions aware of context by capturing temporal dependencies and context information in sequential data. Popular RNN variations with features to address the vanishing gradient issue and identify long-term dependencies in sequential data include Long Short-Term Memory (LSTM) networks and Gated Recurrent Units (GRUs). RNNs are extensively utilized in applications where it's essential to comprehend and generate sequential patterns, like speech recognition, machine translation, and sentiment analysis.

In 2014, Ian Goodfellow unveiled Generative Adversarial Networks (GANs), a revolutionary deep learning system comprising two neural networks developed concurrently through adversarial training: a discriminator and a generator. While the discriminator network learns to differentiate between actual and fake samples, the generator network learns to create synthetic data samples identical to real ones. The generator and discriminator networks develop iteratively through competition in a minimax game, producing realistic and high-quality data samples. GANs have been used for many different tasks, such as data augmentation, style transfer, and image generation, and they have significantly advanced the field of generative modeling.

Neural networks and deep learning models present several difficulties despite their outstanding achievements, such as interpretability problems, vanishing gradients, and overfitting. Poor generalization performance on unseen data results from overfitting, which happens when the model learns to memorize the training data rather than understanding its underlying patterns and structures. To reduce overfitting and enhance neural networks' capacity for generalization, regularization techniques, including dropout, L1 regularization, and L2 regularization, are frequently employed. Vanishing gradients limit the depth of neural networks and impede training by occurring when the gradients of the loss function get too small to update the network's weights. Methods including gradient clipping, batch normalization, and skip connections are employed to overcome vanishing gradients and facilitate the training of more profound and more intricate neural networks.

Another issue with neural networks and deep learning is interpretability; these models frequently function as "black boxes," making comprehending their internal workings and decision-making procedures challenging. To learn the features and patterns that contribute to neural network predictions and obtain insights into neural network behavior, interpretability approaches, including saliency maps, attention processes, and visualization, are employed. To uncover new prospects and applications in data science and artificial intelligence, it will be essential to address these problems and fully utilize neural networks and deep learning as these technologies evolve.

Natural Language Processing

The artificial intelligence and linguistics field of natural language processing, or NLP, aims to make it possible for computers to comprehend, interpret, and produce human language. Natural language processing (NLP) is essential for various applications, such as chatbots, machine translation, sentiment analysis, and information extraction. NLP allows computers to evaluate vast amounts of text data accurately and efficiently.

Tokenization, which includes dividing text into smaller pieces, such as words or sentences, to enable further analysis and processing, is one of the core tasks of natural language processing (NLP). Through tokenization, computers can comprehend natural language's syntax and structure and derive valuable information from textual input.

Part-of-speech tagging is another crucial NLP activity, which entails classifying each word in a sentence with its corresponding part of speech—such as a noun, verb, adjective, or adverb. Part-of-speech tagging helps computers comprehend the relationships between words in a phrase by giving them information about the grammatical structure of sentences. Another NLP problem is named entity recognition (NER), which entails locating and categorizing named entities in text data, including individuals, groups, places, dates, and numerical expressions. Computers may carry out operations like entity linking, information retrieval, and knowledge extraction by using NER to extract pertinent information from text data.

Sentiment analysis is a well-liked use of natural language processing (NLP) that entails examining and categorizing the sentiment or viewpoint conveyed in textual data, including social media posts, product reviews, and consumer feedback. Techniques for analyzing sentiment vary from straightforward ones like bag-of-words models and lexicon-based algorithms to more complex ones like deep learning and neural networks. Businesses can use sentiment analysis to understand consumer sentiment better, spot new trends and issues, and make data-driven decisions to enhance their goods, services, and customer happiness offerings.

Another significant use of NLP is machine translation, which automatically translates text between languages. Machine translation systems employ various methods, including neural, rule-based, and statistical machine translation, to produce precise and natural-sounding translations between languages. By identifying long-range dependencies and semantic correlations in text input, neural machine translation models—based on deep learning and sequence-to-sequence architectures—have attained state-of-the-art performance in machine translation tasks.

Chatbots are artificial conversational agents that comprehend and reply to user requests and questions in natural language using natural language processing (NLP) techniques. Chatbots can be implemented in multiple industries, such as virtual assistants, healthcare, and customer service, to offer tailored and engaging user experiences. Chatbots can perform activities like answering questions, making recommendations, and helping with tasks by using intent recognition, entity extraction, and dialogue management to interpret user inputs and provide relevant responses.

Another significant use of natural language processing (NLP) is information extraction, which removes structured data from unstructured text sources like web pages, reports, and articles. Computers can recognize and extract pertinent entities, relationships, and events from text data using information extraction techniques such as named entity recognition, relation extraction, and event extraction. Businesses and organizations can use information extraction to enhance structured databases with helpful information, automate data entry, and extract insights from unstructured data sources.

NLP is a quickly developing area with many applications and chances for creativity and study. The need for sophisticated NLP methods and solutions will only rise in tandem with the volume and complexity of text data, propelling developments in data science, artificial intelligence, and human-computer interaction.

Businesses, researchers, and organizations can acquire insights into human language and communication, unlock the value of text data, and create intelligent systems and applications that improve productivity, efficiency, and decision-making by utilizing natural language processing (NLP) approaches.

CHAPTER XI

Data Management and Storage

Databases and Data Warehousing

Modern information systems are fundamentally based on data management and storage, which allow organizations to organize effectively and efficiently, store, retrieve, and analyze enormous amounts of data. Two essential elements of data management and storage infrastructure are databases and data warehousing, each of which plays a different role in data processing and management.

Databases are organized collections of structured data that make it easier to manage, change, and retrieve data quickly and effectively. They are the cornerstone for methodically and systematically storing and handling unstructured, semi-structured, and structured data. The most popular database is a relational database, which arranges data into tables with rows and columns and establishes constraints and links between them. The standard language for interacting with relational databases is SQL (Structured Query Language), which allows users to execute several actions, including entering, updating, removing, and querying data.

In contrast, data warehousing is the act of gathering, preserving, and arranging data from many sources to facilitate analytics and business intelligence. Specialized databases called data warehouses are made to hold and analyze vast amounts of historical data, usually from various sources spread throughout an organization. They offer a single repository to unify and standardize the format of data from diverse operational systems, including transactional databases, CRM systems, and ERP systems. Denormalized schemas and dimensional modeling approaches, such as star and snowflake schemas, are frequently used in data warehouses to enhance query performance and enable intricate analytics and reporting.

The ability of data warehouses to facilitate business intelligence and decision-making by offering a sole source of truth for data analysis and reporting is one of its main benefits. Data warehouses facilitate intricate queries and analytics on substantial amounts of historical data, yielding actionable insights and empowering organizations to make well-informed decisions grounded in evidence derived from data analysis. Data warehouses are integrated with business intelligence tools, such as OLAP (Online Analytical Processing) and data visualization software, to allow users to explore and analyze data interactively, produce dashboards and reports, and distribute insights throughout the company.

By offering centralized administration and management of data assets, data warehouses facilitate business intelligence and analytics and play a vital role in data governance and compliance. They impose access rules, security guidelines, and data quality requirements to guarantee the availability, confidentiality, and integrity of data. In addition, data warehouses facilitate data lineage and auditability, which helps businesses monitor the source and use of data, adhere to legal requirements, and reduce the risk of security incidents and data breaches.

Scalability, performance, and cost are just a few of the issues that databases and data warehousing present to businesses despite their advantages. It can be challenging to scale databases and data warehouses to manage rising data quantities and user concurrency; careful planning and architectural design are needed. Performance optimization techniques like indexing, partitioning, and query optimization are crucial to ensure effective data retrieval and processing. Furthermore, the data management and storage infrastructure may be costly in terms of maintenance, licensing, hardware, and software, so businesses must carefully weigh these factors' costs, benefits, and scalability.

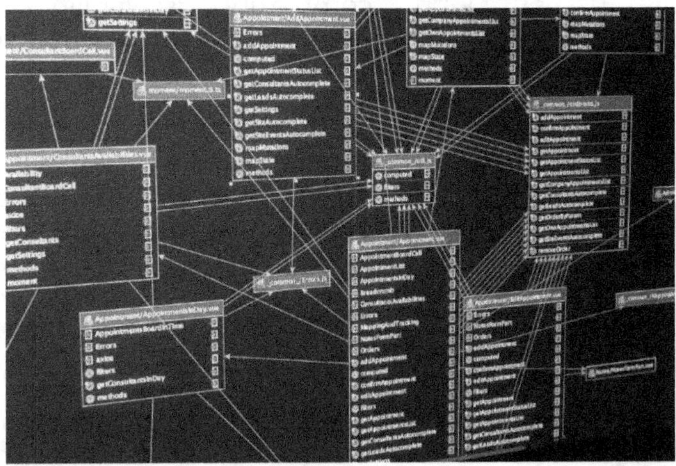

To sum up, databases and data warehousing are crucial elements of contemporary data management and storage infrastructure that allow businesses to organize effectively and efficiently, store, retrieve, and analyze enormous volumes of data. While data warehouses enable firms to combine, consolidate, and analyze data from many sources for business intelligence and analytics, databases are the foundation for storing and managing structured data. Organizations can obtain competitive advantages through data-driven innovation and transformation, get actionable insights, and assist decision-making by utilizing databases and data warehousing. Businesses must also solve scalability, performance, and cost to get the most out of and significantly influence their data management and storage projects.

Big Data Technologies (Hadoop, Spark)

Big data technologies like Hadoop and Spark have completely transformed massive data management, processing, and analysis. These technologies are made to handle issues with complexity, scalability, and performance that come with the exponential development of data. Large datasets can be stored and processed across clusters of commodity hardware using the distributed file system (HDFS) and distributed processing framework (MapReduce) offered by Hadoop, an open-source framework created by the Apache Software Foundation. Organizations can store and analyze petabytes of data cost-effectively and efficiently because of Hadoop's distributed processing and storage capabilities, which use fault tolerance and parallelism to manage various workloads and data types.

Conversely, Spark is a fast, all-purpose cluster computing platform for handling large amounts of data in memory. Spark expands on the MapReduce paradigm with support for in-memory processing and a wide range of high-level APIs for creating scalable and interactive data analysis apps. Spark offers in-memory storage and facilitates interactive and iterative data processing, which sets it apart from Hadoop, which depends on disk-based storage and batch processing. This makes Spark much faster and more adaptable for various use cases, such as machine learning, graph processing, and streaming analytics. Thanks to Spark's unified computing engine, organizations can create end-to-end data pipelines and workflows on a single platform, encompassing data ingestion and preprocessing, model training, and inference.

The ability of Hadoop and Spark to scale horizontally across clusters of commodity hardware is one of their main advantages; it allows enterprises to handle vast volumes of data and support growing workloads and user concurrency. With its fault-tolerant architecture and distributed file system, Hadoop can quickly expand from a few to thousands of nodes, allowing businesses to customize their infrastructure to fit their demands and budgets. Spark is ideally suited for real-time and interactive analytics applications because of its in-memory processing and adequate data caching mechanisms, which allow it to attain even higher levels of scalability and performance.

Support for various data processing and analytics workloads, including batch processing, interactive queries, machine learning, and streaming analytics, is another benefit of Hadoop and Spark. The MapReduce framework in Hadoop is designed to handle massive datasets in batches, which makes it ideal for jobs like data warehousing, log processing, and extract, transform, and load (ETL). In addition to batch processing, Spark's robust ecosystem of libraries and APIs—which includes Spark SQL, MLlib, GraphX, and Spark Streaming—allows it to handle a variety of data-intensive applications, such as interactive SQL queries, graph analytics, machine learning model training, and real-time stream processing.

Moreover, Hadoop and Spark offer strong data integration and communication support with additional analytics and data management tools, allowing businesses to create end-to-end data pipelines and workflows in various heterogeneous contexts. Organizations are given a comprehensive platform for handling and analyzing big data by Apache Hive, Apache Pig, Apache HBase, and Apache Kafka, among other tools and projects for data intake, storage, processing, and analysis that are part of Hadoop's ecosystem. Further enhancing its interoperability and integration possibilities is Spark's support for multiple data formats and sources, including HDFS, S3, Kafka, and JDBC, as well as its compatibility with other data processing frameworks like Hadoop MapReduce and Apache Flink.

To sum up, big data technologies like Hadoop and Spark are solid and adaptable, and they have completely changed how businesses handle, process, and evaluate massive amounts of data. While Spark's in-memory computing engine and rich ecosystem of libraries and APIs enable interactive and real-time analytics on large datasets, Hadoop's distributed file system and MapReduce framework offer scalable and fault-tolerant storage and processing capabilities for batch processing of big data. In today's data-driven world, enterprises can drive innovation and gain a competitive edge by utilizing Hadoop and Spark to harness the value of big data.

Cloud Services for Data Science

Cloud services have entirely changed the discipline of data science by offering scalable, adaptable, and affordable options for storing, processing, and analyzing massive amounts of data. Numerous services and tools are available on cloud computing platforms like Google Cloud Platform (GCP), Microsoft Azure, and Amazon Web Services (AWS) that are especially made for workloads related to data science and analytics. These services include storage options that offer big data and analytics apps scalable and long-lasting storage, like Google Cloud Storage, Amazon S3, and Azure Blob Storage. Using SQL queries and business intelligence tools, cloud-based data warehouses like Amazon Redshift, Azure Synapse Analytics, and Google BigQuery allow enterprises to examine massive amounts of structured data.

Scalability and elasticity are two significant benefits of cloud services for data science, enabling businesses to adjust their infrastructure in response to changes in workload and demand. Cloud computing solutions facilitate dynamic and efficient resource provisioning by offering on-demand access to compute resources, including virtual machines, containers, and serverless activities. This scalability and elasticity are very helpful for data science and analytics workloads, which frequently require substantial computational resources for processing and analyzing massive datasets. Without having to make an initial investment in hardware or equipment, businesses may use cloud services to seamlessly extend their infrastructure to manage increasing data volumes and user concurrency.

AWS Glue, Azure Data Factory, and Google Cloud Dataflow are just a few of the managed data processing and analytics services available through cloud services. These services automate ingesting, transforming, and loading data into analytics platforms. These managed services let businesses quickly and effectively create end-to-end data pipelines and processes by offering pre-built connections and interaction with well-known data sources, including databases, data lakes, and streaming platforms. For distributed data processing and analytics workloads like ETL (extract, transform, load), batch processing, and machine learning model training, cloud-based data processing frameworks like Apache Spark on AWS EMR, Azure HDInsight, and Google Dataproc offer scalable and managed environments.

Additionally, a variety of analytics and machine learning tools and platforms are provided by cloud services, allowing businesses to use their data to create intelligent apps and extract valuable insights. Users may quickly and easily get insights and make data-driven decisions using interactive dashboards and visualizations offered by cloud-based analytics platforms like AWS Quick Sight, Azure Analytics, and Google Data Studio. Without requiring knowledge of infrastructure management or machine learning algorithms, cloud-based machine learning services like AWS SageMaker, Azure Machine Learning, and Google Cloud AI Platform offer managed environments for creating, honing, and deploying machine learning models at scale.

The affordability and pay-as-you-go pricing structure of cloud services, which let businesses pay only for the resources and services they use without requiring upfront capital investments or long-term commitments, is another significant benefit for data scientists. With various price choices, including spot instances, reserved instances, and on-demand pricing, cloud computing platforms help businesses minimize expenses according to workload requirements and usage patterns. This pay-as-you-go pricing model is especially beneficial because data science and analytics workloads frequently involve experimentation, prototyping, and iterative development. It enables enterprises to adjust resources up or down to project needs and budgetary restrictions.

In summary, cloud services are now indispensable tools for data science and analytics because they offer businesses scalable, adaptable, and affordable options for handling, storing, and analyzing massive amounts of data. Organizations may quickly develop intelligent apps, automate workflows for data processing, obtain meaningful insights from data, and grow their infrastructure dynamically by utilizing cloud services. Cloud services will become more crucial as data volume and complexity increase in helping businesses realize the value of their data, spur innovation, and gain a competitive edge in today's data-driven economy.

CHAPTER XII

Data Visualization and Reporting

Tools for Data Visualization (Tableau, Power BI)

Transforming raw data into insightful and helpful information requires visualization tools like Tableau and Power BI. These technologies help organizations produce visually appealing and interactive dashboards, charts, and reports that facilitate compelling user exploration, analysis, and communication of data insights. Leading data visualization software Tableau from Tableau Software offers a robust and user-friendly platform for building interactive dashboards and visualizations from various data sources. Tableau's drag-and-drop interface and various visualization choices allow users to quickly create visually stunning visualizations without requiring much coding knowledge or technical proficiency.

Microsoft's Power BI is another well-liked data visualization tool that lets users generate interactive dashboards and reports from various data sources, including spreadsheets, databases, and cloud services. In addition to offering a recognizable and user-friendly interface for creating and sharing visualizations, Power BI interfaces effortlessly with other Microsoft products, including Excel, Azure, and SQL Server. Power BI's extensive data modeling features enable users to carry out intricate computations, data transformations, and analytics on massive datasets, allowing organizations to gain actionable insights and make decisions based on data.

One of Tableau and Power BI's main advantages is connecting to and visualizing data from various sources, such as databases, spreadsheets, cloud services, and big data platforms. Users can access and analyze data from numerous sources on a single platform using these technologies, including connectors and interfaces with like SQL databases, Excel spreadsheets, Salesforce, Google Analytics, and Hadoop. Organizations may obtain a holistic understanding of their data and reveal insights that might not be seen from individual datasets alone by utilizing Tableau and Power BI to integrate data from different sources.

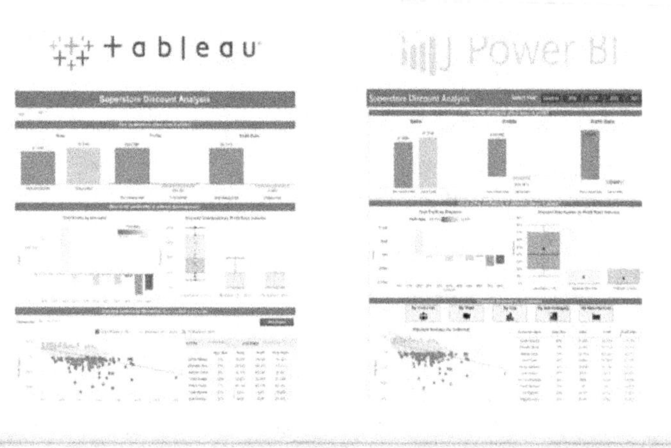

Additionally, Tableau and Power BI include various customization choices and visualization options, enabling users to construct highly personalized and interactive visuals that satisfy their unique requirements. A vast array of chart formats, including scatter plots, bar charts, line charts, histograms, and heat maps, are available with these tools, along with sophisticated functions like drill-down, filtering, and dynamic parameters. Users may develop visually appealing and educational dashboards and reports that effectively communicate findings and engage stakeholders thanks to Tableau and Power BI's versatile design and customization choices.

Thanks to Tableau and Power BI's support for collaboration and sharing, users can effortlessly share reports, dashboards, and visualizations with stakeholders, clients, and coworkers. Tableau Online and Tableau Server offer centralized platforms for safely publishing and disseminating Tableau workbooks and visualizations to users inside or outside an enterprise. Similarly, Power BI provides Power BI Report Server, an on-premises tool for organizing and distributing Power BI material within an organization, and Power BI Service, a cloud-based platform for publishing and sharing Power BI analyses and dashboards.

In conclusion, companies may turn raw data into valuable insights and eye-catching representations using Tableau and Power BI, two solid and adaptable data visualization technologies. Tableau and Power BI enable users to successfully explore, analyze, and share insights from data thanks to their user-friendly interfaces, extensive customization possibilities, and reliable connectivity options. In today's data-driven world, companies may promote innovation and growth, make better decisions, and obtain a deeper understanding of their data by utilizing these technologies.

Creating Interactive Dashboards

A key component of data visualization is the creation of interactive dashboards, which help businesses display complex data in an exciting and user-friendly way. With interactive dashboards, users can efficiently explore, analyze, and engage with data to obtain insights and make data-driven decisions. Understanding the audience's needs and preferences and building dashboards that meet their unique needs is one of the fundamentals of developing interactive dashboards. The dashboard design must be adjusted to reflect the essential metrics, KPIs (key performance indicators), and data points pertinent to the target audience.

When designing interactive dashboards, it's critical to prioritize simplicity and clarity, making sure that the layout is user-friendly and straightforward. Logical data organization, clear labels and titles, and user-friendly navigation controls like drill-downs, tooltips, and filters help users locate information quickly and comprehend the dashboard's insights. Consistent usage of design components, such as typefaces, color schemes, and visual styles, can also improve the dashboard's overall user experience and give it a more polished, eye-catching appearance.

Building interactive dashboards requires selecting the appropriate chart types and visualization strategies to communicate data insights effectively. Depending on the data's nature and the audience's tastes, different chart types, including bar charts, line charts, pie charts, and scatter plots, may be more appropriate for presenting particular types of data and relationships. Cluttered or deceptive visualizations that could confuse or mislead viewers should be avoided in favor of chart formats that most properly and clearly express the desired message.

Moreover, interactivity is a crucial component of interactive dashboards that lets users explore and evaluate data dynamically. Clickable buttons, dropdown menus, sliders, and hover-over tooltips are examples of interactive elements that enable users to engage with the dashboard and go deeper into particular data points or interest areas. Additionally, dynamic filtering and highlighting should be supported by interactive dashboards so that users may easily explore various viewpoints and scenarios and concentrate on pertinent data.

Performance optimization and scalability are critical factors to consider when building interactive dashboards to guarantee responsive and seamless user experiences, especially when working with big datasets or intricate visualizations. Enhancing dashboard efficiency and responsiveness can help users interact with the dashboard more effectively by caching frequently requested data, decreasing data transfer, and optimizing data queries. Furthermore, utilizing server-side processing, caching methods, and pre-aggregated data can assist interactive dashboards in scaling better and meeting rising user concurrency and workload needs by lessening the strain on backend systems.

Finally, iteration and user feedback are crucial for creating dynamic dashboards that satisfy users' changing needs and preferences. Usability testing, user feedback, and design iterations based on user insights and input are all recommended to increase the usability, efficacy, and adoption of interactive dashboards over time. Interactive dashboards' long-term viability and utility in promoting data-driven decision-making and organizational success depend on the constant monitoring and enhancement of dashboard performance, usability, and user engagement.

Storytelling with Data

In data visualization and analytics, the ability to successfully convey insights and discoveries to a variety of audiences through storytelling with data is a crucial skill for analysts and data scientists. Fundamentally, data storytelling entails creating an engaging tale around the data and utilizing context, narratives, and visualizations to make points, elicit feelings, and motivate action. A fundamental tenet of data-driven storytelling involves comprehending the target audience and crafting a tale that speaks to their needs, interests, and preferences. This is structuring the story in a way that interests and captivates the audience, in addition to recognizing the essential ideas, insights, and takeaways pertinent to them.

Concentrating on simplicity and clarity when using statistics to convey a story is crucial so that it's simple to read and comprehend. Audiences may find complex data and analysis overwhelming. Therefore, it's critical to condense the information into straightforward, understandable statements. Employing basic visual aids like maps, graphs, and charts can aid in demystifying challenging ideas and improving the audience's ability to interact with and comprehend the material. Furthermore, giving the audience background information and justifications for the data and insights offered can aid in directing them through the story and successfully reinforcing essential points.

Using narratives and visuals to evoke a feeling of storytelling and establish an emotional bond with the audience is another facet of data storytelling. Anecdotes, examples, and real-world situations are examples of storytelling strategies that analysts can use to inject life into the data and make it more accessible and exciting for the audience. Employing visual components like hues, forms, and visuals can also aid in evoking feelings and producing an unforgettable and powerful narrative. Ultimately, using statistics to make captivating stories that connect with the audience personally is more important than just presenting facts and figures when motivating action and bringing about change.

Furthermore, properly guiding the audience through the data and insights through a logical and cohesive narrative is critical to data-driven storytelling. This entails organizing the story logically, beginning with an introduction that establishes the background and goals, understandably presenting the facts and analysis, and concluding with a conclusion that highlights the most critical findings and ramifications. Storytelling frameworks like the hero's journey or the three-act structure can be used to create a captivating narrative arc that keeps the audience interested and immersed in the story.

Storytelling with data requires creating an exciting tale, actively involving the audience, and promoting interaction and engagement. Interactive visualizations that let consumers explore the data and find insights on their own, including clickable charts and dashboards, can help achieve this. Opportunities for audience questions, comments, and conversations can also promote a collaborative and interactive storytelling experience. This will allow analysts and audience members to co-create the narrative and jointly provide fresh ideas and viewpoints.

Last, using data to tell stories is an iterative process that calls for constant development and tinkering depending on audience input and observations. Analysts can gradually improve the efficiency and impact of their storytelling endeavors by gathering feedback, testing usability, and adjusting the story and visuals in response to audience input. When new information and insights become available, audience preferences and demands change, and storytelling with data must be constantly learning and adapting. By adopting a data-driven storytelling methodology and continuously improving their storytelling abilities, analysts may craft captivating stories that stimulate action, propel transformation, and significantly influence their institutions and societies.

CHAPTER XIII

Business and Finance

Predictive Analytics in Business

In today's data-driven world, predictive analytics is vital for companies looking to gain a competitive advantage. Using historical data, statistical algorithms, and machine learning approaches, predictive analytics helps organizations foresee changes, spot opportunities, and take proactive decision-making by forecasting future trends, behaviors, and results. Predictive modeling, which entails creating statistical models and algorithms to predict future events or behaviors based on historical data, is one of the primary uses of predictive analytics in business. Companies may more effectively manage resources, optimize inventories, and reduce risks by using these models to predict client demand, sales trends, market circumstances, and other essential business variables.

Customer analytics, which analyzes customer data to find patterns, trends, and preferences that may be utilized to tailor marketing campaigns, raise customer satisfaction levels, and boost customer retention, is another significant use of predictive analytics in business. Organizations can customize their marketing efforts and customer experiences to individual requirements and preferences by using predictive models to classify customers based on their behavior, forecast customer attrition, and promote personalized products or offers. By utilizing predictive analytics, businesses can increase revenue and profitability by anticipating client demands, sending tailored messages, and cultivating enduring customer connections.

Predictive analytics is also frequently utilized in the financial services industry for fraud detection and risk management. Organizations can detect and stop fraudulent activities like credit card fraud, identity theft, and money laundering by using predictive models to examine transaction data, customer behavior, and other pertinent characteristics to identify potential risks and abnormalities. Financial institutions can efficiently manage risk exposure and make data-driven lending decisions that balance reward and risk because of these models' ability to evaluate credit risk, forecast loan defaults, and optimize lending decisions.

Predictive analytics also significantly benefit firms in the supply chain management domain by streamlining production planning, transportation, and inventory control. Utilizing previous sales data, supplier performance, demand projections, and other information, predictive models can forecast future demand, spot possible bottlenecks, and improve distribution networks and inventory levels. Organizations may avoid stockouts, cut down on excess inventory, and enhance supply chain efficiency by utilizing predictive analytics, ultimately lowering costs and increasing customer satisfaction.

Predictive analytics is also increasingly utilized in human resources for workforce planning, talent management, and employee retention. Organizations may efficiently attract, develop, and retain top people using predictive models to assess employee data, performance metrics, and other pertinent criteria. These models can also identify high-potential employees, forecast attrition, and suggest retention tactics. Additionally, by predicting staffing needs, identifying skill shortages, and optimizing workforce allocation, these models can assist firms in creating resilient and adaptable teams essential to their business' success.

In the current competitive business environment, predictive analytics has shown to be an effective tool for companies looking to gather insights, optimize operations, and spur growth. Organizations may forecast future trends, behaviors, and outcomes using historical data, statistical algorithms, and machine-learning approaches. This allows them to proactively discover opportunities, anticipate changes, and make well-informed decisions. Predictive analytics has several uses and advantages for companies in various sectors, including risk management, labor planning, inventory optimization, and personalization of marketing campaigns. Predictive analytics will become more crucial as data volume and complexity increase to assist businesses in realizing the value of their data and fostering innovation and success in the digital era.

Risk Management and Fraud Detection

A vital component of corporate operations, risk management, and fraud detection are essential in sectors like finance, insurance, and retail, where there is a high risk of financial loss from fraud or unanticipated circumstances. While fraud detection focuses on spotting and stopping fraudulent activity like theft, embezzlement, or financial fraud, risk management manages, evaluates, and mitigates risks that could affect an organization's goals, operations, or financial performance. Data analysis, statistical modeling, and machine learning approaches are used in risk management and fraud detection to find patterns, anomalies, and trends pointing to possible hazards or fraudulent activity.

The overwhelming amount and complexity of data that firms must examine to spot possible hazards and fraud trends is one of the main obstacles to risk management and fraud detection. Conventional techniques for managing risks and detecting fraud, like rule-based systems and manual audits, are frequently labor-intensive, time-consuming, and prone to human error. But thanks to data analytics and machine learning developments, firms can now automate and expedite the risk management and fraud detection process. This is done using massive amounts of data to find patterns and abnormalities pointing to possible dangers or fraudulent activity.

Because predictive analytics helps firms predict future patterns, behaviors, and results based on historical data, it is essential to risk management and fraud detection. Predictive models can examine patterns, correlations, and linkages in the data to spot possible dangers or fraud trends and forecast upcoming occurrences or actions. Predictive models, for instance, can be used in the financial services sector to identify potential hazards, like credit defaults or market volatility, and take preemptive steps to reduce them by analyzing transaction data, client behavior, and market patterns. Predictive models can also be used in retail to discover possible fraud tendencies, such as odd purchase patterns or questionable transactions, and flag them for more investigation. These models can examine sales data, inventory levels, and consumer behavior.

To find patterns and abnormalities in the data, machine learning techniques, including supervised learning, unsupervised learning, and deep learning, are also widely employed in risk management and fraud detection. Organizations can identify and stop fraud in real-time using supervised learning algorithms trained on labeled data to classify transactions as legitimate or fraudulent. Conversely, unsupervised learning algorithms can analyze massive amounts of unlabeled data, which can then find patterns and anomalies that might point to fraud or other possible hazards. Organizations can uncover and stop sophisticated fraud schemes by using deep learning algorithms, such as neural networks, to examine complicated, high-dimensional data and find subtle patterns and correlations that human analysts may miss. Furthermore, advanced analytics techniques like text mining, social network analysis, and network analysis are also employed in risk management and fraud detection to find hidden patterns and linkages in the data. Network analysis tools can examine the relationships and exchanges between various organizations, including clients, transactions, and accounts, to spot possible fraud rings or organized criminal networks. To spot any cooperation or insider threats, social network analysis techniques can examine the interactions and social ties between people. Text mining algorithms can identify possible dangers or fraudulent actions, such as fraudulent claims or suspicious communications, by analyzing unstructured data, such as text documents or consumer feedback.

Risk management and fraud detection are essential tasks for businesses looking to safeguard their resources, reduce financial losses, and uphold stakeholder confidence. Organizations can anticipate future events or behaviors, identify potential risks and fraud tendencies, and take proactive steps to mitigate such risks and stop fraudulent acts by utilizing data analytics, statistical modeling, and machine learning approaches. Predictive analytics and machine learning will play a more significant part in risk management and fraud detection as the volume and complexity of data continue to rise. This will help organizations avoid new threats and successfully defend their interests.

Customer Segmentation and Personalization

Segmenting and personalizing clients are crucial tactics for companies trying to comprehend and meet their clientele's varied demands and preferences. While customer personalization entails adjusting products, services, and marketing messages to each customer based on their distinct characteristics and preferences, customer segmentation entails dividing customers into discrete groups based on common characteristics, such as demographics, behavior, or preferences. These approaches rely on advanced analytics techniques, machine learning, and data analysis to find patterns, trends, and insights that help businesses properly segment their client base and provide tailored experiences that increase engagement and loyalty.

One of the main advantages of customer segmentation is that it makes it easier for businesses to recognize and comprehend various client groups, which allows them to customize their offerings in terms of goods, services, and marketing initiatives to each group's unique requirements and preferences. Through customer segmentation based on demographic factors like age, gender, income, or geography, businesses can learn more about the traits and preferences of various consumer segments and create promotions and marketing efforts that appeal to them. Similarly, behavioral segmentation—based on browsing habits, purchase history, and engagement level—allows businesses to pinpoint high-value clients, spot upselling and cross-selling opportunities, and enhance customer acquisition and retention campaigns.

Additionally, businesses can better deploy resources and capital to optimize return on investment by identifying and ranking their most valued consumers. Organizations can determine which of their clients are the most profitable by segmenting their customer base according to variables like lifetime value, frequency of purchases, or level of involvement. Then, they can concentrate on keeping and upselling to those consumers. Optimizing the value of their current client base can assist businesses in enhancing customer retention, raising customer lifetime value, and stimulating revenue development.

Contrarily, personalization elevates customer segmentation by offering customized recommendations and experiences to each customer based on their distinct tastes, actions, and interactions with the business. Businesses can personalize marketing messages, product recommendations, and content across various channels, including emails, mobile apps, and websites, using data analytics, machine learning, and artificial intelligence to predict customer preferences and analyze customer data. Organizations may boost customer engagement, encourage conversions, and cultivate enduring customer relationships by providing tailored experiences.

The requirement to gather, combine, and evaluate massive amounts of data from multiple sources to understand consumer behavior and preferences is one of the main obstacles to customer segmentation and customization. Organizations must use data management platforms, CRM systems, and advanced analytics tools to effectively collect and analyze customer data and uncover patterns, trends, and insights that inform segmentation and personalization strategies. Additionally, to safeguard consumer data and guarantee the moral and responsible use of data in segmentation and customization initiatives, enterprises must ensure compliance with data protection rules, such as the CCPA and GDPR.

Moreover, a customer-centric strategy that prioritizes comprehending and satisfying each customer's wants and preferences is necessary for customer segmentation and customization. To learn about consumers' preferences, problems, and expectations entails getting input from them, conducting surveys and interviews, and monitoring their interactions and behaviors. By knowing their customers' requirements and preferences, organizations may create tailored experiences and suggestions that enhance the customer journey, foster trust and loyalty, and set the brand apart in a crowded market.

In summary, customer segmentation and personalization are crucial tactics for businesses looking to comprehend and interact with their clients meaningfully. Organizations can customize their goods, services, and marketing initiatives to match individual consumers' unique requirements and preferences by segmenting their customer base based on shared traits and behaviors, offering personalized experiences and recommendations, and increasing customer engagement, loyalty, and revenue. To help organizations deliver seamless and personalized experiences that delight customers and drive business success, data analytics, machine learning, and advanced analytics techniques will play an increasingly important role in customer segmentation and personalization as the volume and complexity of customer data continue to grow.

CHAPTER XIV

Healthcare and Medicine

Medical Image Analysis

The study of developing and using computer methods to extract valuable data from medical images, such as X-rays, MRIs, CT scans, and ultrasound images, is known as medical image analysis. To examine interior structures and organs non-invasively and detect anomalies or diseases, medical imaging is essential for diagnosing, treating, and managing a wide range of medical disorders. Medical image analysis tools automatically analyze and interpret medical pictures, supporting radiologists and clinicians in making precise diagnoses and treatment decisions. These approaches use sophisticated algorithms, machine learning, and artificial intelligence.

Computer-aided diagnosis (CAD), which entails creating algorithms and systems to help radiologists and clinicians evaluate medical pictures and identify anomalies or diseases, is one of the primary uses of medical image analysis. CAD systems use a combination of feature extraction, image processing, and machine learning algorithms to evaluate medical pictures, identify regions of interest (such as tumors, lesions, or fractures), and send alerts or recommendations for diagnosis to medical personnel. CAD systems have been created for various medical imaging modalities, such as radiography, neuroimaging, and mammography. It has been demonstrated that these systems increase the efficiency and accuracy of diagnostic interpretation, which can result in early illness diagnosis and treatment.

Additionally, image segmentation—the process of breaking down medical images into discrete areas or structures of interest, such as organs, tissues, or lesions—is a typical application of medical image analysis in research. Measurement of volumes or areas of interest, study, quantification of anatomical structures, and feature extraction for research or diagnostics depend on image segmentation. Medical image segmentation algorithms employ various approaches, including edge detection, region expanding, and thresholding, to identify the borders between multiple structures precisely. Applications for segmentation techniques can be found in oncology, neurology, and cardiology, among other medical specialties. These techniques help researchers understand how diseases progress, how treatments respond, and how patients fare.

Medical image analysis is also utilized in image registration to identify anatomical changes, monitor the course of a disease, or schedule surgical procedures, which entails aligning and comparing several medical images of the same patient or different patients. Image registration methods enable quantitative analysis of spatial correlations and differences between images by employing mathematical transformations, such as deformable models or affine transformations, to align medical photos precisely. With image registration techniques, medical personnel can make better decisions and achieve better patient outcomes in various operations, including radiation planning, image-guided surgery, and longitudinal research.

Medical image analysis is utilized in imaging equipment for picture reconstruction, noise reduction, artifact correction, and diagnosis and research. Using mathematical algorithms and signal processing techniques, image reconstruction algorithms create medical images from raw data obtained by imaging modalities, such as magnetic resonance imaging (MRI) or computed tomography (CT). These algorithms seek to increase diagnostic accuracy, decrease noise and artifacts, and improve image quality by recreating high-resolution images from low-resolution or noisy data. Image reconstruction techniques are essential to enhance the functionality and efficiency of medical imaging equipment and provide healthcare practitioners with high-quality images for precise diagnosis and treatment planning.

To sum up, medical image analysis is a quickly developing subject that is essential to contemporary healthcare since it helps medical practitioners to efficiently examine, analyze, and interpret medical pictures for study, treatment, and diagnosis. Medical image analysis techniques can potentially transform medical imaging and improve patient outcomes by enabling earlier detection, more accurate diagnosis, and tailored treatment planning. These approaches are made possible by using modern algorithms, machine learning, and artificial intelligence. Medical image analysis will play a more prominent and significant role in the healthcare industry as the number and complexity of medical imaging data continue to rise, allowing medical professionals to utilize medical imaging for better patient care and results fully.

Predictive Models for Patient Care

By utilizing data analytics, machine learning, and artificial intelligence to predict patient outcomes, identify high-risk people, and customize treatment strategies, predictive models for patient care are transforming the healthcare sector. Large volumes of patient data, such as imaging studies, demographic data, test results, and medical histories, are analyzed by these models to find patterns, trends, and correlations that can assist healthcare professionals in making better decisions and enhancing patient outcomes.

Risk stratification, which entails identifying patients at high risk of developing specific medical illnesses or experiencing adverse outcomes, such as hospital readmissions, complications, or mortality, is one of the primary uses of predictive models for patient care. Predictive models examine patient data by identifying risk variables like comorbidities, chronic illnesses, or demographic traits and computing a risk score or likelihood of unfavorable outcomes. By prioritizing interventions, allocating resources, and customizing treatment plans to the needs of high-risk patients, healthcare professionals can use these risk scores to lower costs and enhance patient outcomes.

Predictive models are also utilized in patient care to tailor interventions and treatment plans to each patient's unique needs, preferences, and therapeutic outcomes. These models evaluate patient data to determine the best course of therapy, dose schedules, and care plans that are customized to meet the unique requirements and preferences of every patient. Healthcare professionals may provide individualized care that maximizes effectiveness and avoids side effects by using predictive analytics and machine learning to forecast how patients react to various treatments and interventions.

Predictive models for patient care are utilized for early medical condition identification and intervention, risk stratification, and customized treatment planning. To enable healthcare providers to intervene early and stop or postpone the advancement of the disease, these models evaluate patient data to discover subtle indications and symptoms that may suggest the onset of a medical condition or disease progression. Predictive models, for instance, can use data from electronic health records (EHRs) to identify patients who, due to a combination of lifestyle factors, genetic predispositions, and medical history, are at high risk of developing diabetes or heart disease. This allows healthcare providers to take preventive measures, like medication therapy or lifestyle changes, to reduce the likelihood of complications.

Additionally, by anticipating patient demand, resource use, and capacity requirements, predictive models for patient care are utilized to optimize resource allocation and healthcare delivery. These models estimate future demand and identify potential bottlenecks or capacity restrictions by analyzing previous data on patient volumes, acuity levels, and resource consumption trends. Healthcare professionals can use these projections to improve staffing levels, bed distribution, and treatment scheduling. This will help to guarantee that resources are used effectively and that patients receive timely, affordable care.

In conclusion, by enabling more proactive, individualized, and effective patient treatment, predictive models for patient care can potentially revolutionize healthcare delivery. Healthcare professionals can use artificial intelligence, machine learning, and data analytics to evaluate large volumes of patient data to optimize resource allocation, forecast results, and tailor treatment programs. This ultimately improves patient outcomes and lowers healthcare costs. Predictive models will play a more significant part in patient care as predictive analytics develops. They help healthcare practitioners provide high-quality, patient-centered care that adapts to patients' and healthcare systems' changing requirements and preferences.

Genomic Data Analysis

At the nexus of biology, genetics, and data science, the rapidly expanding area of genomic data analysis aims to decode the immense quantity of genetic information recorded inside an individual's DNA. Billions of DNA base pairs comprise the human genome, which contains information on a person's inherited characteristics, propensity for disease, and reaction to medical interventions. Processing, evaluating, and interpreting genetic data is known as genomic data analysis, and it is done to understand human health, disease causes, and personalized therapy.

The discipline of precision medicine, which seeks to customize medical interventions and treatments to each patient's unique traits, including their genetic composition, is one of the primary uses for genomic data analysis. Researchers and medical professionals can predict disease risk, diagnose genetic disorders, and determine the best course of treatment for individual patients by analyzing genomic data to find genetic variants, mutations, and biomarkers linked to particular diseases or conditions. In contrast to conventional chemotherapy, targeted medicines based on the precise genetic abnormalities causing cancer patients' tumors have been developed thanks to genomic data analysis, which has improved treatment outcomes and decreased side effects.

Additionally, genomic data analysis is employed in genetic research to find new therapeutic targets, investigate the genetic causes of disorders, and create novel medication targets. Using genomic data, researchers use genome-wide association studies (GWAS) to find genetic variations linked to particular diseases or behaviors. Researchers can learn more about disease mechanisms, find possible drug targets, and create novel therapeutic approaches for illness prevention or treatment by examining the genetic architecture of diseases. Using genomic data analysis has yielded noteworthy progress in comprehending intricate illnesses like cancer, diabetes, and cardiovascular ailments. Additionally, it has facilitated the creation of tailored therapies and precision medicine methodologies.

Genomic data analysis is used in clinical genetics to identify and treat genetic illnesses, hereditary conditions, and disease research and drug discovery. Using genomic sequencing technologies and genetic testing, medical professionals can examine a patient's DNA to find genetic variations that might cause hereditary illnesses or disorders. Healthcare professionals can identify genetic abnormalities, evaluate an individual's and their family member's risk for disease, and offer individualized recommendations for disease management, screening, and prevention by examining genomic data. Clinical genetics has undergone a revolution thanks to genomic data analysis, allowing medical professionals to give patients and their families individualized treatment and counseling for those with genetic illnesses.

Additionally, population genetics uses genomic data analysis to investigate human groups' evolutionary history and genetic diversity. Researchers can examine genetic variants, population migrations, and evolutionary adaptations that have sculpted the genetic landscape of humanity by studying genomic data from various communities worldwide. Studies on population genetics shed light on humans' evolutionary history, migration patterns, genetic diversity, and possible connections to health and illness. The genetic foundation of human migration, the genesis of hereditary diseases, and the genetic variety of contemporary human populations are just a few of the ground-breaking population genetics findings made possible by studying genomic data.

To sum up, genomic data analysis is an effective technique that helps scientists and medical professionals decipher the mysteries of the human genome and learn more about human health, illness, and evolution. By evaluating genomic data, researchers can find genetic variants, pinpoint illness risk factors, and create individualized therapies and interventions that enhance patient outcomes. The field of genomic data analysis will play an increasingly significant role in biology, medicine, and personalized medicine as genomic sequencing technologies progress and the volume of genomic data increases. This will help shape the future of healthcare and advance our understanding of the genetic basis of health and disease.

CHAPTER XV

Social Media and Marketing

Sentiment Analysis

Sentiment analysis, often known as opinion mining, is a natural language processing technique that examines text material to detect the sentiment or emotion portrayed in it. Sentiment analysis provides significant insights into public opinion, consumer feedback, and brand impression in an era where massive amounts of textual data are generated regularly via social media, customer reviews, news stories, and other sources. The purpose of sentiment analysis is to categorize text as good, harmful, or neutral, allowing businesses to understand public sentiment better, assess customer satisfaction, and make data-driven decisions.

One of the most common applications of sentiment analysis is social media monitoring, in which corporations examine user-generated content on platforms such as Twitter, Facebook, and Instagram to understand better public opinion and sentiment toward their brand, products, or services. Organizations may spot patterns, monitor brand sentiment in real time, and predict potential issues or crises by analyzing social media posts, comments, and mentions before they escalate. Organizations can use social media sentiment research to better communicate with their audience, handle customer problems, and manage their online reputation.

Furthermore, sentiment analysis is commonly used in market research to assess consumer feedback and reviews, assisting businesses in understanding customer happiness, identifying emerging trends, and gaining competitive insights. Analyzing product evaluations, survey replies, and customer feedback forms allows firms to find improvement areas, analyze customer sentiment changes over time, and compare their performance to competitors. Sentiment analysis enables businesses to make data-driven decisions, prioritize product innovations, and customize marketing campaigns to client demands and preferences.

In addition to brand monitoring and market research, sentiment analysis is utilized in financial markets to assess investor sentiment and forecast market trends by analyzing news stories, press releases, and social media activity. Financial analysts can discover market sentiment indicators such as optimism, pessimism, or uncertainty by analyzing textual data from financial news sources, social media platforms, and investor forums and incorporating them into their trading strategies. Sentiment analysis enables investors to make better judgments, forecast market trends, and efficiently manage investment risks.

Sentiment analysis is also used in customer care and support to evaluate client interactions, including emails, chat transcripts, and help requests, to better understand consumer sentiment and resolve issues. By evaluating customer feedback and sentiment, organizations can identify reoccurring issues, prioritize support efforts, and adjust replies to suit their customers' requirements and expectations. Sentiment analysis enables firms to give individualized and proactive customer care, increasing customer satisfaction and loyalty.

Sentiment analysis is also used in political analysis to assess public opinion and attitudes toward political candidates, parties, and policies. Political analysts can use social media posts, news stories, and public remarks to evaluate popular opinion, identify critical problems, and follow changes in voter sentiment over time. Sentiment analysis allows political campaigns to better identify voter preferences, modify messaging, and target outreach efforts, influencing electoral outcomes.

To summarize, sentiment analysis is a powerful tool that allows enterprises to evaluate and understand text data, acquire insights into public opinion, and make data-driven decisions across multiple domains. Organizations can track brand sentiment, assess consumer feedback, forecast market trends, improve customer service, and inform political tactics by evaluating sentiment in social media posts, customer reviews, news stories, and other textual data sources. As the volume and variety of textual data grows, sentiment analysis will play an increasingly essential role in developing company strategies, informing decision-making, and understanding human behavior.

Targeted Advertising

Targeted advertising is a marketing approach that involves delivering targeted advertisements to certain groups of consumers based on their demographics, interests, behavior, or other attributes. As opposed to traditional mass advertising, targeted advertising employs data analytics, machine learning, and artificial intelligence to segment audiences and present customized messages that speak to each person's needs and interests. With this strategy, advertisers can increase the efficacy of their marketing initiatives, optimize their advertising campaigns, and get better returns on investment.

Reaching the right audience with the right message at the right time increases the likelihood of engagement and conversion, one of the main benefits of targeted advertising. By examining consumer data, including browsing history, purchasing patterns, and demographic details, advertisers can pinpoint niche audiences most likely to be interested in their offerings. Advertisers can then adapt their commercials to appeal to these audience segments, delivering individualized messages that address their specific requirements, preferences, and interests. The advertising campaign is more effective overall, and the commercials are more relevant due to this tailored strategy.

Furthermore, by concentrating their efforts on the most profitable and relevant audience segments, advertisers can maximize their advertising budgets through targeted advertising. Advertisers can target their ads to specific audience segments that are more likely to become customers, saving money on mass advertising campaigns that may reach a big but irrelevant population. Through more effective resource allocation, advertisers can attain excellent conversion rates, sales, and income while optimizing the return on investment of their advertising expenditure.

Targeted advertising increases efficiency and targeting and makes it possible for marketers to measure and track campaign effectiveness more precisely. In real-time, advertisers may measure essential performance metrics like impressions, clicks, conversions, and return on investment by utilizing data analytics and advertising technology platforms. With this fine-grained level of information, marketers can track the success of their ads, fine-tune their language and targeting tactics, and make data-driven choices that will enhance campaign performance over time.

Moreover, targeted advertising allows marketers to present relevant and customized advertising experiences through various platforms and channels, including email, social media, mobile apps, and websites. By merging data from several sources and channels, advertisers may provide a unified and consistent advertising experience for customers, irrespective of their device or location. By engaging customers at several touchpoints along the customer journey, advertisers can increase brand knowledge, consideration, and loyalty through an omnichannel strategy.

However, targeted advertising also brings up issues with customer privacy, data security, and morality. Advertisers risk breaking data protection laws and violating consumer privacy rights as they gather and analyze ever-increasing customer data to target ads more efficiently. By getting customers' express agreement before collecting and utilizing their data for targeted advertising, advertisers can guarantee compliance with privacy laws and regulations, such as the California Consumer Privacy Act (CCPA) and the General Data Protection Regulation (GDPR).

To sum up, targeted advertising is an effective marketing tactic that helps companies reach particular audience segments with tailored messages, maximize their spending on advertising, track the effectiveness of their campaigns, and provide seamless advertising experiences across various platforms. Advertisers may improve the relevancy and efficacy of their advertising campaigns, resulting in increased engagement, conversion, and return on investment, by utilizing data analytics, machine learning, and advertising tech platforms. To maintain targeted advertising's integrity, civility, and compliance with relevant laws and regulations, advertisers must also handle issues about customer privacy, data protection, and ethical considerations.

Trend Analysis and Forecasting

In many businesses, trend analysis and forecasting are crucial for examining past data, spotting patterns, and projecting future trends. Organizations can obtain critical insights into customer behavior, market dynamics, and business performance by looking at historical trends and patterns in data. This helps them create plans that will work for them in the future and make well-informed decisions.

Finding and comprehending patterns and trends in data across time is one of the main goals of trend analysis. Companies can discern seasonal patterns, long-term trends, and recurrent patterns that could impact future results by examining past data, including sales numbers, market shares, and website traffic. By using trend analysis, organizations may monitor and comprehend the underlying variables behind changes in essential metrics and indicators, such as revenue growth, client acquisition, or product demand. Organizations may foresee changes in the market, seize new opportunities, and reduce risks and obstacles by recognizing trends early on.

In addition, trend analysis allows companies to predict future trends and outcomes using historical data. Using statistical methods like machine learning algorithms, regression analysis, and time series analysis, companies can create predictive models that forecast future values of critical metrics or indicators and extrapolate historical trends. Through forecasting, businesses can more effectively manage resources, plan inventory levels, and create marketing plans by predicting future demand, sales volumes, or market trends. Organizations can make proactive decisions that set them up for success in a business climate that is changing quickly by utilizing trend analysis and forecasting.

In the financial markets, trend analysis and forecasting are used to assess stock prices, bond yields, and other economic indicators to spot investment opportunities, control associated risks, and project future trends. Investors and financial analysts can find patterns, correlations, and anomalies pointing to possible buying or selling opportunities by examining past price data and market movements. Using forecasting techniques like econometric modeling and technical analysis, investors can anticipate future price changes and use this information to decide when to purchase, sell, or hold onto their investments. When making investing decisions, trend analysis and forecasting are essential tools that assist investors in managing erratic markets and reaching their financial objectives.

In supply chain management, trend analysis and forecasting are also used to optimize distribution networks, production schedules, and inventory levels. Organizations can estimate future demand for products or components and detect patterns and trends in supply and demand by evaluating past demand data, lead times, and supply chain performance metrics. By forecasting, businesses can reduce the risk of stockouts and excess inventory by planning production and procurement activities of demand fluctuations. Trend analysis and forecasting ensure that the correct products are available in the right quantities at the right times, helping businesses optimize their supply chain operations, cut costs, and increase customer satisfaction.

Firms must overcome the constraints and difficulties associated with trend research and forecasting to ensure accuracy and dependability. Past data won't always anticipate future patterns, particularly in volatile or quickly evolving markets. External variables that can affect future results and add uncertainty to forecasting models include the economy's state, regulations changes, and technological improvements. Inaccuracies and errors in forecasting can also result from problems with the data quality, assumptions made by the model, or unforeseen occurrences that should be considered during the study. Organizations must constantly review and update their forecasting models to increase the accuracy of their forecasts and adjust to shifting market conditions.

To sum up, trend analysis and forecasting are valuable techniques businesses use to examine past data, spot trends, and project future trends across various industries. Using trend analysis and forecasting methodologies, organizations can obtain critical insights into customer behavior, market dynamics, and corporate performance. This helps them formulate effective future strategies and make well-informed decisions. Even though trend analysis and forecasting have limitations and difficulties, businesses can get past these by constantly improving their models, adding fresh data, and adjusting to shifting market conditions. Ultimately, this helps companies to succeed and remain competitive in a fast-paced business environment.

CHAPTER XVI

Government and Public Policy

Data-Driven Decision Making

Data-driven decision-making is a strategy approach that uses data analysis and insights to guide business decisions and create organizational performance. In today's digital age, firms collect massive amounts of data from various sources, such as customer interactions, transactions, operations, and market trends. Organizations can use data analytics, machine learning, and business intelligence tools to find patterns, trends, and correlations in their data, providing essential insights into their business operations, consumer behavior, and market dynamics.

One of the primary advantages of data-driven decision-making is its capacity to increase decision accuracy and efficacy. Organizations can make more informed and objective data-driven decisions by relying on factual evidence and quantitative analysis rather than intuition or gut feeling. Whether it's optimizing marketing campaigns, pricing tactics, or supply chain operations, data-driven decision-making helps firms find opportunities, reduce risks, and allocate resources more effectively, resulting in improved business outcomes.

Furthermore, data-driven decision-making helps firms better understand their customers and marketplaces. Organizations can segment their customer base, identify target audiences, and tailor marketing messages and services by evaluating consumer data such as demographics, preferences, and purchase history. Similarly, by assessing market data and trends, businesses can uncover new possibilities, anticipate changes in customer behavior, and stay ahead of the competition in a fast-changing market.

In addition to enhancing decision accuracy and consumer insights, data-driven decision making can increase operational efficiency and cost reduction. Organizations can uncover inefficiencies, bottlenecks, and opportunities for improvement by reviewing operational data such as production indicators, inventory levels, and supply chain performance. Data-driven insights enable firms to streamline operations, optimize resource allocation, and decrease waste, resulting in cost savings and increased organizational productivity.

Furthermore, data-driven decision-making allows firms to monitor and analyze performance against key performance indicators (KPIs) and corporate objectives. Establishing explicit measurements and benchmarks will enable firms to track progress, identify areas of underperformance, and take corrective action to address issues and enhance performance. Data-driven insights give organizations real-time access to their performance, allowing them to make proactive decisions and course corrections to stay on track and meet their goals.

However, implementing a data-driven decision-making culture requires firms to overcome several obstacles, including data silos, data quality difficulties, and cultural reluctance to change. Many organizations face fragmented data sources and heterogeneous systems, making accessing, integrating, and analyzing data effectively tricky. Furthermore, guaranteeing data quality and reliability is critical for making accurate judgments; moreover, many businesses need help with data cleanliness, consistency, and completeness. Furthermore, cultural resistance to change and dependence on old decision-making processes might impede the implementation of data-driven decision-making within firms.

To summarize, data-driven decision-making is an effective strategy that allows businesses to use data analytics and insights to influence business decisions, drive organizational performance, and achieve a competitive advantage in today's data-driven environment. Organizations that embrace data-driven decision-making can enhance accuracy, get deeper customer insights, increase operational efficiency, and monitor and track performance against corporate objectives. While establishing a data-driven decision-making culture is complex, firms that effectively embrace it benefit significantly in terms of agility, competitiveness, and long-term success in a quickly changing business environment.

Urban Planning and Smart Cities

Most people now live in cities, so urban planning and intelligent cities are important ideas today. Urban planning entails designing, developing, and managing cities and communities to guarantee sustainable growth, adequate infrastructure, and a high standard of living for citizens. Conversely, intelligent cities use innovation, data, and technology to solve urban problems and improve urban areas' efficiency, sustainability, and livability.

Creating well-designed, livable, and inclusive cities and communities is one of the main objectives of urban planning. To build dynamic and resilient urban settings that satisfy the demands of a diverse population, urban planners strive to balance several aspects, including housing, transportation, green areas, and public services. Urban planners can create comprehensive plans and policies that direct the development and evolution of cities sustainably and equitably by interacting with stakeholders, carrying out research, and evaluating data.

Intelligent cities elevate urban planning to a new level by combining technology and data-driven solutions to address urban challenges and enhance citizens' quality of life. Innovative city projects gather and analyze data on various urban issues, including waste management, energy consumption, traffic congestion, and air pollution. They utilize sensors, Internet of Things (IoT) devices, and data analytics. Using data and technology, smart cities can increase service delivery, manage urban infrastructure, and boost operational efficiency.

Furthermore, intelligent cities encourage resilience and sustainability in urban settings by utilizing innovation and technology. Smart cities can lessen the effects of climate change, reduce carbon emissions, and conserve natural resources by constructing energy-efficient buildings, deploying renewable energy sources, and streamlining transportation systems. Additionally, intelligent city projects concentrate on improving disaster preparedness and response capabilities by utilizing real-time data and predictive analytics to foresee and lessen the consequences of calamities and natural disasters.

To support a robust and competitive urban economy, intelligent cities prioritize innovation and economic development in addition to sustainability and resilience. Smart cities may draw in talent, encourage innovation, and boost economic growth by investing in digital infrastructure, encouraging entrepreneurship, and supporting innovation hubs. Creating possibilities for digital inclusion and fair access to resources and technology is another primary goal of innovative city projects, which ensure that everyone can take advantage of the opportunities presented by the digital economy.

Additionally, to guarantee that urban development is responsive to citizens' needs and ambitions, intelligent cities prioritize citizen engagement and participation in decision-making processes. Smart cities help businesses, communities, and government agencies communicate, collaborate, and co-create using digital platforms and technology. Urban planning and decision-making procedures incorporate citizen feedback and input, allowing cities to address local objectives, issues, and preferences transparently and inclusively.

The shift to smart cities is not without difficulties, though, as there are hazards related to cybersecurity, digital inequality, and privacy. There are worries over data security and privacy and the possibility of personal data being misused as intelligent cities collect and analyze large volumes of data from sensors and Internet of Things (IoT) devices. Furthermore, a barrier to fair access to technology and digital services is the digital gap that still exists across urban and rural areas and inside cities. Moreover, the susceptibility of intelligent cities to cybersecurity threats and attacks emphasizes the necessity of solid cybersecurity rules and measures to safeguard vital data and infrastructure.

To sum up, smart cities and urban planning are essential for influencing how cities develop and raising living standards for locals. Cities may become more resilient, sustainable, and inclusive by incorporating technology, data, and innovation into the processes involved in urban planning and decision-making. While there are many chances for innovation and economic growth in intelligent cities, obstacles must be overcome to guarantee that the advantages of technology and data-driven solutions are distributed fairly and that cities continue to be resilient, safe, and safe in an increasingly digital world.

Public Health Analysis

Public health analysis is critical in guaranteeing the safety and well-being of communities and populations. It entails the methodical gathering, analysis, and interpretation of health-related data to find patterns, trends, and risk factors that affect public health outcomes. Public health analysis greatly influences policies, programs, and interventions to avoid diseases, boost health, and enhance the general quality of life for people and communities.

Monitoring and evaluating population health is one of the main goals of public health analysis. Public health analysts can determine health disparities, assess the disease burden, and identify regions that need to be prioritized for intervention by gathering and evaluating data on various health indicators, including disease prevalence, death rates, and health habits. By gaining knowledge about how health outcomes vary among different demographic groups—including age, gender, race, ethnicity, socioeconomic status, and geography—public health analysis helps policymakers and medical professionals focus resources and interventions where they are most needed.

Furthermore, identifying outbreaks and disease surveillance depend heavily on public health analysis. By monitoring risk factors, transmission patterns, and disease incidence, public health analysts can uncover new risks, stop the spread of infectious illnesses, and spot outbreaks early. Disease surveillance systems gather information from various sources, including hospitals, labs, and public health organizations. They then apply analytical methods, like geographic analysis and epidemiological modeling, to find trends, patterns, and clusters that might point to a threat to the public's health.

Public health analysis is used to assess the efficacy of public health treatments and programs, in addition to disease surveillance. By evaluating programs, tracking key performance indicators, and reviewing program outcomes, public health analysts can ascertain whether interventions are accomplishing their intended goals and improving public health outcomes. Program evaluation entails gathering data on program inputs, activities, outputs, and outcomes to determine the efficacy, efficiency, and sustainability of public health interventions. Analytical techniques, such as cost-effectiveness analysis and outcome evaluation, are then used.

Moreover, local, national, and international policy creation and decision-making depend heavily on public health analysis. Public health analysts can advocate for policies and programs that promote health equality, address the social determinants of health, and identify policy gaps and opportunities by delivering evidence-based data and analysis to policymakers on the health needs and priorities of communities. To improve health outcomes and lessen health disparities, public health analysis is essential in formulating public health policies that address disease prevention, health promotion, environmental health, and healthcare delivery.

However, public health analysis must overcome several obstacles, including poor data quality, privacy concerns, and more resources for data collection and analysis. Public health data's completeness, accuracy, and timeliness can vary since they are frequently gathered from various sources, including administrative records, surveys, healthcare facilities, and registries. Data quality problems can impact the validity and reliability of the findings of public health analyses. These problems include missing or incomplete data, inconsistent data, and input errors.

When gathering, examining, and disseminating health data, public health analysts also have to navigate moral and legal issues regarding data privacy and confidentiality. Maintaining individual privacy and confidentiality is crucial in public health analysis, particularly when handling sensitive health data. Ensuring the responsible and secure handling of personal health information is contingent upon public health analysts adhering to ethical norms and data protection rules.

In summary, public health analysis offers data-driven insights into health status, disease patterns, and health outcomes, making it an essential tool for enhancing population health and well-being. Public health analysts can track health trends, identify epidemics, assess interventions, shape policy, and support evidence-based tactics that advance health equality and deal with social determinants of health through collecting, analyzing, and interpreting health data. Public health analysis is crucial in guiding public health decisions and enhancing health outcomes, even if it encounters data quality, privacy, and resource limitations.

CHAPTER XVII

Ethics in Data Science

Data Privacy and Security

Data privacy and security are critical issues in the digital age. Due to the widespread use of data gathering, storage, and sharing technologies, there are more opportunities for unwanted access, misuse, and exploitation of personal information. While data security entails preventing unauthorized access, alteration, or destruction of data, data privacy protects individuals' personal information from unauthorized use, disclosure, or access. Maintaining trust and confidence in digital systems and services and guaranteeing data confidentiality, integrity, and availability depend on both ideas.

The gathering and use of enormous volumes of personal data by businesses and service providers is a paramount data privacy and security issue. Digital technology and the Internet of Things (IoT) have enabled enterprises to gather and examine vast amounts of data from various sources, including social media platforms, mobile apps, websites, and sensors. Although this data can help organizations get valuable insights and enhance service delivery, it also raises questions regarding the security and privacy of people's data. Organizations must abide by data protection laws and regulations, such as the California Consumer Privacy Act (CCPA) and the General Data Protection Regulation (GDPR), which mandate that they implement strong security measures to prevent personal information from being accessed, disclosed, or misused and that they obtain individuals' explicit consent before collecting and using that data.

Furthermore, the frequency with which identity theft, cyberattacks, and data breaches occur highlights how crucial data security is to protecting private information from malevolent parties and online dangers. Cybersecurity risks include phishing attacks, malware, ransomware, and insider threats. These threats can seriously jeopardize an organization's data assets and result in monetary losses, reputational harm, and legal ramifications. Organizations must implement thorough cybersecurity measures, like encryption, access controls, multi-factor authentication, and frequent security audits and assessments, to reduce these risks and safeguard data against theft, illegal access, and exploitation.

Organizations need to manage internal risks and vulnerabilities that could jeopardize data security and privacy in addition to external threats. Insider threats can seriously endanger the security and integrity of data. These dangers might come from careless workers, malevolent insiders, or human error. In addition to educating staff members about data privacy and security best practices, organizations must have policies, processes, and training programs in place to reduce the risk of insider threats. These measures include access limits, user education, and the monitoring and auditing user activity.

In addition, new difficulties and complications in data privacy and security have been brought about by the quick uptake of cloud computing, big data analytics, and Internet-connected gadgets. Through cloud computing, businesses can process and store data on distant servers and data centers, providing scalability, flexibility, and financial savings. However, since data may be processed and stored in several places across various jurisdictions with disparate data protection rules and regulations, it also presents questions regarding data residency, jurisdiction, and control. Similarly, massive data analytics and Internet of Things (IoT) devices produce enormous amounts of data that might contain sensitive information like financial transactions, location data, or personal health records. This raises questions about data security and privacy risks related to data aggregation, analysis, and sharing.

Furthermore, the growing interconnection of digital systems and services and emerging technologies like machine learning (ML) and artificial intelligence (AI) present new opportunities and problems for data privacy and security. Thanks to AI and ML technologies, organizations may now study and gain insights from massive datasets, but there are worries about algorithmic bias, discrimination, and privacy issues. Organizations must deploy privacy-enhancing technologies like federated learning, homomorphic encryption, and differential privacy to safeguard sensitive data while promoting data analysis and innovation.

In conclusion, data privacy and security are crucial issues in the digital age, with the gathering, processing, and sharing of personal data becoming more commonplace in daily life. By putting robust data protection mechanisms in place, adhering to data protection laws and regulations, and educating stakeholders and employees about data privacy and security best practices, organizations may demonstrate their commitment to protecting sensitive data. Organizations may reduce the risks of data breaches, cyberattacks, and regulatory non-compliance and foster trust and confidence among partners, consumers, and staff by protecting data privacy and security. Ultimately, this ensures the confidentiality, integrity, and accessibility of data in the digital age.

Ethical Considerations in AI and ML

Since artificial intelligence (AI) and machine learning (ML) continue to influence many facets of society, such as healthcare, banking, transportation, and employment, ethical considerations in these fields are critical. Systems utilizing AI and ML can significantly improve productivity, automate time-consuming chores, and improve decision-making. However, they also raise moral issues related to prejudice, accountability, transparency, and justice.

Equitable treatment and fairness rank among the most critical ethical factors in AI and ML. Since historical data is used to train AI and ML algorithms, it may contain biases and inequalities that exist in society. AI and ML systems may reinforce or even worsen already-existing inequalities and prejudice against specific groups, such as women, marginalized communities, and ethnic minorities if these biases are not addressed. To reduce prejudice and guarantee that AI and ML systems treat people equally and impartially, regardless of their demographic features, fairness-aware algorithms and fairness metrics can be helpful.

Moreover, accountability and openness are ethical factors in AI and ML. Holding AI and ML systems responsible for their acts and comprehending how they make decisions can become more complex as these systems grow more complicated and independent. By offering insights into the decision-making processes of AI and ML systems and pointing out potential sources of bias, error, or unintended consequences, explainable AI (XAI) techniques and transparency measures, such as model documentation, auditing, and monitoring, can help increase the transparency and accountability of these systems.

Furthermore, as AI and ML technologies frequently collect, process, and analyze substantial amounts of personal data, privacy is a primary ethical concern in these fields. Techniques for maintaining privacy, such as differential privacy, encryption, and data anonymization, can help safeguard people's right to privacy and make sure that private information is not disclosed or misused.

Organizations must also abide by data protection laws and regulations, such as the California Consumer Privacy Act (CCPA) and the General Data Protection Regulation (GDPR), which mandate that they get individuals' consent before collecting and using their data and that they put in place the necessary security measures to protect that data from disclosure or unauthorized access.

Moreover, interpretability and transparency are ethical issues in AI and ML. It can be challenging to comprehend how AI and ML systems make decisions and interpret their results as they grow more complicated and opaquer. This lack of transparency can erode faith in AI and ML systems, particularly in high-stakes applications like healthcare, finance, and criminal justice. Explainable AI (XAI) approaches, which give users insight into the decision-making processes of AI and ML systems and make their outputs understandable and reliable, can contribute to an increase in the transparency and interpretability of these systems. Examples of these approaches include feature importance analysis, model visualization, and post-hoc explanation methods.

In addition, accountability and responsibility are ethical factors in AI and ML. Establishing procedures for holding AI and ML systems responsible for their deeds and results is crucial as these systems get increasingly independent and capable of making decisions without human input. This includes creating standards and guidelines for the ethical development and application of AI and ML, clearly outlining the roles and duties of developers, users, and stakeholders, and putting procedures in place for recourse and redress if AI and ML systems cause harm or wrongdoing.

Furthermore, societal effects and unforeseen consequences are ethical problems in AI and ML. While AI and ML systems provide hazards and issues that need to be appropriately evaluated and solved, they can also significantly improve society. Stakeholder engagement, participatory approaches, and ethical impact assessments can all help identify potential risks, trade-offs, and unintended consequences of deploying AI and ML and ensure that these technologies are developed and used in a way that aligns with human values, ethical principles, and social norms.

In conclusion, ethical issues in AI and ML are critical to ensuring that these technologies are created and applied in a way that upholds the dignity and well-being of people and communities. Organizations may increase trust and confidence in AI and ML systems, reduce risks and damages, and optimize the advantages of these technologies for society at large by addressing concerns with fairness, accountability, transparency, privacy, and bias. To develop and execute ethical frameworks, norms, and standards that support ethical AI and ML development, and deployment, technologists, ethicists, policymakers, and stakeholders must collaborate in a multidisciplinary manner.

Responsible Data Science Practices

Ensuring that data-driven decision-making processes are carried out ethically, transparently, and in a way that respects people's rights, privacy, and dignity requires responsible data science methods. Organizations must emphasize ethical data science practices in the age of big data and machine learning to reduce possible risks and harms related to data collection, analysis, and usage. The Principles and factors included in responsible data science are data governance, accountability, openness, fairness, and privacy.

Data governance is a fundamental concept in responsible data science that pertains to establishing guidelines, protocols, and controls for gathering, archiving, and applying data. Organizations may assure compliance with data protection rules and regulations, define clear roles and responsibilities, and set data quality standards using data governance frameworks. Organizations may reduce the risk of data breaches, illegal access, and misuse while fostering stakeholder confidence and trust by implementing robust data governance procedures.

Furthermore, in data-driven decision-making processes, responsible data science methods prioritize accountability and openness. Transparency entails disclosing in an understandable and readily available manner the procedures and algorithms used to gather, process, and utilize data, as well as the data analysis and decision-making algorithms. Holding people and organizations accountable for their data science-related actions and decisions includes ensuring that choices are just, morally sound, and consistent with societal standards and organizational ideals. Organizations may cultivate a culture of ethical data use and decision-making and increase trust and confidence in their data science methods by encouraging accountability and openness.

Fairness and equity are also prioritized in ethical data science practices while developing and implementing data-driven systems and algorithms. If AI and machine learning algorithms are designed without considering the effects on various population groups or if they are trained on biased data, they may create bias and discrimination. To practice responsible data science, businesses must prioritize the interests and rights of disadvantaged and vulnerable people, ensure that decision-making processes are fair and equitable, and uncover and remove biases in data and algorithms.

Furthermore, ethical data science practices place a high priority on privacy and data protection, making sure that personal data about individuals is gathered, processed, and utilized in compliance with relevant laws and rules, including the California Consumer Privacy Act (CCPA) and the General Data Protection Regulation (GDPR). Techniques that improve privacy, like data anonymization, encryption, and differential privacy, can lessen the likelihood that personal data will be misused, accessed without authorization, or disclosed. Organizations may demonstrate their commitment to responsible data usage and management and gain the trust and confidence of customers, employees, and other stakeholders by prioritizing privacy and data protection.

Furthermore, responsible data science methods encourage ethical decision-making and professional behavior among data scientists, guaranteeing that they follow moral guidelines and standards. Honesty, integrity, respect for people's rights and privacy, and consideration of possible effects on society and the environment are among the ethical factors in data science. To minimize risks and guarantee that their work is carried out ethically and responsibly, data scientists must consider their possible risks and implications, including the possibility of harm, unforeseen outcomes, and ethical issues.

Ethical, transparent, and respectful data-driven decision-making procedures that uphold people's rights, privacy, and dignity depend on responsible data science techniques. Organizations can reduce risks and harms associated with data collection, analysis, and usage and cultivate a culture of ethical data use and decision-making by prioritizing principles like data governance, transparency, accountability, fairness, and privacy. Data scientists, legislators, ethicists, and stakeholders must work together to create and execute ethical frameworks, rules, and standards that support responsible data use and management across businesses and industries.

CHAPTER XVIII

Implementing Data-Driven Strategies

Building Data-Driven Cultures in Organizations

In today's data-driven world, where data plays a significant role in decision-making, innovation, and competitive advantage, developing data-driven cultures within enterprises is imperative. A data-driven culture values data incorporates it into decision-making processes and uses it to shape plans, policies, and actions at all organizational levels. To effectively leverage the power of data and achieve business outcomes, a data-driven culture must be fostered through leadership, organizational alignment, technical skills, and change management tactics.

Leadership is crucial in establishing and promoting a data-driven culture in organizations. Senior leaders must demonstrate a clear vision for data-driven decision-making and emphasize the strategic value of data in meeting corporate goals and objectives. Leaders can set an example by incorporating data-driven approaches into their decision-making processes and investing in data literacy training and development for staff at all levels of the organization. Leaders may instill trust and confidence in employees by demonstrating a commitment to data-driven ideas and practices, laying the groundwork for a data-driven culture to thrive.

Furthermore, establishing a data-driven culture necessitates alignment and collaboration across departments and functions. Silos and obstacles between business groups can make it difficult to share data, collaborate, and align goals and objectives. Organizations must break down these barriers and establish a culture of cooperation and knowledge sharing to enable data-driven decision-making throughout the firm. Cross-functional teams, data governance committees, and collaborative projects can aid in aligning and integrating data and insights across departments and functions, allowing businesses to use data more effectively to achieve shared goals and objectives.

Furthermore, developing technical skills is critical for allowing staff to collect, analyze, and understand data to drive decision-making and innovation. Organizations must invest in data infrastructure, tools, and technologies that enable employees to access, analyze, and visualize data effectively. Data literacy training and development programs can assist employees in developing the skills and abilities required to effectively deal with data and generate insights that inform decision-making processes. Organizations may enable workers to be more data-driven in their work and decision-making by developing technological capabilities and cultivating a continual learning and development culture.

Furthermore, developing a data-driven culture necessitates focusing on change management tactics to overcome resistance to change and encourage the adoption of data-driven practices and behaviors. Change management strategies, like communication campaigns, training programs, and organizational incentives, can assist in educating employees about the advantages of data-driven decision-making while also addressing concerns and misconceptions regarding the use of data in decision-making processes. Leaders must foster an environment that supports experimentation, creativity, and learning from data-driven insights while giving people the resources and support required to thrive in their data-driven activities.

Furthermore, establishing a data-driven culture necessitates emphasizing diversity, equity, and inclusion to ensure that data-driven decision-making processes are fair, unbiased, and reflect varied viewpoints and experiences. Organizations must be aware of the possibility of bias and discrimination in data and algorithms and take proactive steps to address these issues through diversity and inclusion initiatives, bias detection and mitigation techniques, and continuous monitoring and evaluation of data-driven decision-making processes. By supporting diversity, equity, and inclusion, organizations may guarantee that data-driven decision-making processes are ethical, transparent, and consistent with organizational values and societal standards.

Finally, developing data-driven cultures in organizations involves a combination of leadership, organizational alignment, technical capabilities, and change management methods to harness the power of data and deliver business outcomes effectively. Organizations may unleash new potential for innovation, growth, and competitive advantage by cultivating a culture that values data, incorporates it into decision-making processes, and uses it to inform strategies and actions at all levels. Building a data-driven culture is an ongoing process that involves dedication, effort, and constant development; however, a data-driven organization's benefits are enormous in enhanced decision-making, operational efficiency, and organizational performance.

Overcoming Challenges in Data Science Projects

Data science initiatives have enormous potential for extracting essential insights from data to drive corporate decisions, improve processes, and spark innovation. However, they do present some hurdles that can stymie progress and success. Overcoming these problems necessitates a combination of technical competence, organizational support, strategic planning, and good project management tactics.

Data quality and availability are among the most significant issues in data science projects. Data may be partial, inconsistent, or of low quality, making extracting valuable insights and making accurate forecasts difficult. Data scientists frequently spend significant time cleaning, preparing, and validating data before using it for analysis and modeling. Organizations must invest in data governance practices, quality assurance processes, and infrastructure to ensure that data is accurate, reliable, and easy to analyze.

Furthermore, more apparent objectives and stakeholder agreement are significant issues in data science projects. Data science projects may fail to generate value if they are not in line with the organization's strategic goals and objectives or if stakeholders have competing priorities or expectations. Organizations must identify clear objectives, scope, and success criteria for data science projects and involve stakeholders early and frequently to ensure alignment and support. Design thinking workshops, stakeholder interviews, and user input sessions are examples of collaborative methodologies that can assist organizations in identifying business needs, prioritizing requirements, and defining project objectives and deliverables.

Technological complexity is a prevalent issue in data science initiatives, especially when dealing with vast, heterogeneous, and unstructured datasets or adopting advanced machine learning algorithms and methodologies. Data scientists must have the technical competence and domain knowledge to choose relevant approaches, algorithms, and tools for data analysis and modeling. They should also be able to overcome technological issues and restrictions that may develop throughout the project's lifetime. To address this, organizations must engage in ongoing learning and development initiatives to build a professional data science workforce capable of addressing difficult technological challenges and fostering innovation.

Furthermore, resource restrictions, such as a restricted budget, time, and expertise, can be significant obstacles in data science efforts. Data science projects necessitate substantial investments in technology, infrastructure, and human capital and devoted time and effort to collect, clean, and analyze data, create models, and validate results. Organizations must prioritize resources, manage budgets, and acquire leadership sponsorship and support to ensure that data science projects have the resources and financing they require to thrive. Furthermore, enterprises may consider utilizing external talent, such as consulting firms, academic institutions, or freelancing data scientists, to enhance internal competencies and overcome resource limitations.

Furthermore, company culture and aversion to change might impede the acceptance and implementation of data science initiatives. Data-driven decision-making may challenge existing organizational processes, practices, and hierarchies, necessitating cultural and attitude adjustments to accept data-driven approaches. Organizations must establish an environment of creativity, experimentation, and continuous improvement to overcome reluctance to change and encourage the adoption of data-driven processes. Leadership support, staff training, and development, as well as communication and change management techniques, can assist firms in overcoming cultural obstacles and creating an environment conducive to data-driven decision-making and innovation.

In conclusion, data science projects encounter hurdles that might impede progress and success. Overcoming these problems necessitates a combination of technical competence, organizational support, strategic planning, and good project management tactics. In today's data-driven world, organizations can unlock the full potential of data science projects by addressing challenges such as data quality, stakeholder alignment, technical complexity, resource constraints, and organizational culture. Data science projects have hurdles, but with the appropriate approach and mindset, businesses can overcome them and achieve the transformative power of data-driven decision-making and creativity.

Future Trends and Innovations in Data Science

The future of data science is brimming with potential, poised to revolutionize how organizations harness data to drive business outcomes, foster creativity, and tackle complex challenges. As technology advances and data volumes surge, a multitude of significant themes are shaping the future of data science, including strides in artificial intelligence (AI), machine learning (ML), data analytics, and data-driven decision-making.

One of the most impactful trends in data science is the continuous evolution of AI and machine learning technology. AI and machine learning algorithms are growing in power and capability, handling complex tasks like natural language processing, image recognition, and predictive analytics with astounding accuracy and efficiency. As AI and machine learning progress, organizations are utilizing them to automate processes, personalize consumer experiences, optimize operations, and glean new insights from data. Moreover, the democratization of AI and ML tools and platforms is empowering organizations of all sizes and industries to harness the power of AI and ML, driving innovation and gaining a competitive edge in the market.

Another significant development in data science is the growing use of data analytics and business intelligence (BI) technologies to extract meaningful insights from data and drive data-driven decisions. Data analytics solutions are becoming more intuitive, user-friendly, and accessible, enabling business users to explore, analyze, and visualize data without requiring deep technical knowledge. Organizations are using data analytics and business intelligence tools to understand better customer behavior, market trends, and business performance, allowing them to make more informed decisions and adapt faster to changing market dynamics. Furthermore, integrating advanced analytics approaches such as predictive modeling, prescriptive analytics, and real-time analytics allows firms to forecast future trends better, discover opportunities, and manage risks.

Furthermore, the development of big data and the Internet of Things (IoT) drives data science innovation by creating massive amounts of data from various derivations, including sensors, devices, and social media platforms. Big data technologies, such as Hadoop, Spark, and NoSQL databases, enable enterprises to store, process, and analyze enormous amounts of data quickly and affordably, opening up new avenues for data-driven innovation and discovery. Furthermore, incorporating IoT devices and sensors into products, processes, and services generates real-time data streams that organizations can use to monitor performance, optimize operations, and facilitate decision-making in various industries, including manufacturing, healthcare, transportation, and retail.

Furthermore, the convergence of data science with other emerging technologies, including blockchain, edge computing, and quantum computing, accelerates innovation and creates new opportunities for data-driven applications and solutions. Blockchain technology, for example, enables enterprises to share and verify data across widespread networks securely. In contrast, edge computing allows for real-time data processing and analysis at the network's edge, closer to the data source.

Additionally, quantum computing can alter data science by performing complex calculations and simulations that are beyond the capabilities of traditional computing systems, revealing new insights and discoveries in fields such as drug discovery, materials science, and climate modeling.

As data science advances, ethical considerations and responsible AI are taking center stage, reflecting the ongoing struggle with issues of bias, fairness, transparency, and accountability in AI and ML algorithms and decision-making processes. With the increasing prevalence and influence of AI and ML technologies in society, companies are compelled to prioritize ethical considerations and implement responsible AI policies. This ensures that AI and ML systems are developed and deployed in a manner that is fair, transparent, and accountable. This includes the use of fairness-aware algorithms, explainable AI methodologies, and ethical principles and standards for AI and machine learning development and deployment.

To summarize, future developments and innovations in data science hold enormous promise for delivering economic value, promoting innovation, and addressing complex challenges in today's data-driven society. Advances in AI, machine learning, data analytics, big data, IoT, and other technologies are creating new opportunities for businesses to use data to obtain insights, make educated decisions, and create value for customers, employees, and stakeholders. Furthermore, ethical considerations and responsible AI are becoming increasingly relevant as organizations work to develop and deploy AI and ML systems that are fair, transparent, and accountable. Organizations that embrace these trends and breakthroughs can realize data science's full potential for driving innovation, accelerating growth, and creating a better future for all.

CONCLUSION

As we conclude our exploration of "Mastering Data Science and Analytics: The Power of Data: From Analysis to Action in the Modern World," we reflect on the transformative journey we have embarked upon together. Throughout these pages, we've delved into the intricate world of data science and analytics, uncovering how data can drive innovation, inform decision-making, and shape the future of industries worldwide.

From laying the groundwork with foundational concepts to mastering advanced analytical techniques, you have demonstrated a remarkable ability to navigate the complexities of the data landscape. This is not the end of our journey together, but the beginning of a new chapter in your data-driven endeavors, a testament to your hard work and dedication.

As you step forward into the world beyond these pages, remember that the true power of data lies not in its mere existence but in how it is wielded. Whether you are leading a team of data scientists, guiding organizational strategy, or simply seeking to make a difference in your corner of the world, remember that every data point holds the potential to ignite significant change, and you are the catalyst.

We encourage you to recommence exploring, experimenting, and innovating with data, always mindful of your work's ethical implications and societal impacts. By harnessing the power of data responsibly and ethically, you can shape a brighter, more data-driven future for us all.

Thank you for buying and reading/listening to our book. If you found this book useful/helpful please take a few minutes and leave a review on the platform where you purchased our book. Your feedback matters greatly to us.

www.ingramcontent.com/pod-product-compliance
Lightning Source LLC
Chambersburg PA
CBHW072006170726

47999CB00013B/463

9 798330 219124